DOVER · THRIFT · EDITIONS

The United States Constitution

The Full Text with Supplementary Materials

Edited and with
Supplementary Materials by

Bob Blaisdell

DOVER PUBLICATIONS, INC.
Mineola, New York

DOVER THRIFT EDITIONS

GENERAL EDITOR: MARY CAROLYN WALDREP

EDITOR OF THIS VOLUME: JANET BAINE KOPITO

Copyright

Copyright © 2009 by Dover Publications, Inc.
All rights reserved.

Bibliographical Note

The United States Constitution: The Full Text with Supplementary Materials is a new compilation of materials from standard editions, first published by Dover Publications, Inc., in 2009. A new Introduction and notes (appearing throughout in italics), have been specially prepared for this Dover edition by Bob Blaisdell. The documents contained in this compilation reflect the minor errors, omissions, and inconsistencies of the original texts, which also include some archaic usages.

Library of Congress Cataloging-in-Publication Data

United States.
  [Constitution]
  The United States Constitution : the full text with supplementary materials / edited and with supplementary materials by Bob Blaisdell.
    p. cm.
  "A new compilation of materials from standard editions, first published by Dover Publications, Inc., in 2009 . . . A new Introduction and notes . . ."
  Includes bibliographical references.
  ISBN-13: 978-0-486-47166-2
  ISBN-10: 0-486-47166-7
  1. Constitutions—United States. 2. Constitutional law—United States. 3. Constitutional history—United States. I. Blaisdell, Robert. II. Title.
  KF4525 2009
  342.7302'3—dc22
                                                2009011753

Manufactured in the United States by Courier Corporation
47166702
www.doverpublications.com

INTRODUCTION

The making of the Constitution is one of the most satisfying of American stories: through a summer's worth of debates and arguments in Philadelphia at the Constitutional Convention of 1787, the delegates presented to the states — and to history — the most effective national legal document ever created. "The American Constitution has functioned and endured longer than any other written constitution of the modern era. It imbues the nation with energy to act, at the same time restraining its agents from acting out of line," writes the scholar Richard B. Morris. "Above all, the Constitution is the mortar that binds the fifty-state edifice under the concept of federalism, the unifying symbol of a nation composed of many millions of people claiming different national origins, races, and religions."[1]

The Declaration of Independence (1776) and the Revolutionary War pulled the former thirteen British colonies together, but even before the war's end in 1783, their alliance was stretched thin, and individual states looked out for themselves — associated but not tied together except catch-as-catch-can. George Washington, as commander in chief of the armies, was continually frustrated by the haphazard funding provided by the Continental Congress. After the war, the various states proceeded to govern themselves as independent entities. Most of the states had adopted constitutions of their own, many of them inspired by that of John Adams in Massachusetts, with state governments being essentially legislative bodies. In some states, governors were elected by legislators who came up for election every year. There was thus active, immediate participation by voters, within each state; however, the ease of making and unmaking laws was not necessarily

---

[1] Richard B. Morris. *Witnesses at the Creation: Hamilton, Madison, Jay and the Constitution.* New York: Henry Holt. 1985. 3.

balanced, for instance, by long-term goals, executive oversight, or judicial review. Government was local and idiosyncratic, each state pursuing its own way, issuing its own money, sometimes absolving itself or its citizens of debts owed to other states or countries.

When discussion of a central and national government arose in the mid-1780s, many of those who had fought for liberty from the British were not inclined to place their states in subjection to a larger, less responsive government, and yet, the free-flowing, uncoordinated governance of the states seemed to be leading to chaos. Could there be too much liberty? General Washington feared a factionalized, disintegrated, economically uncoordinated nation in which war among the states would be inevitable. In September of 1786, James Madison, a member of the Virginia House of Delegates, who would become the fourth president of the United States in 1809, called for an economic summit to "remedy the defects of the federal government," and although only five states sent representatives, Alexander Hamilton of New York was among them, and he suggested the meeting that became the Constitutional Convention.

Madison, who had conducted research on republican governments, studiously prepared for the convention and made it possible for vital work to be done in that long hot Philadelphia summer of 1787. His "Virginia Plan," presented by Virginia's governor and convention delegate Edmund Randolph, got the proceedings under way on May 29, and this plan formed the rough draft of the Constitution. The discussions at the Convention were secret, permitting participants to debate freely and with few inhibitions about the evolution of their ideas about the nation's governance. The biggest debate, according to Madison, was not *whether* there would be a new central government, but how the power among the larger and smaller populated states would be balanced. The "Great Compromise" of July 16 settled that arrangement: each state would be represented by two senators but with proportional representation according to population in the larger house. George Washington, whose attendance at the convention automatically gave it weight, was elected to preside over the fifty-five delegates, and while he was usually silent in his role, America's other world-famous citizen, eighty-one-year-old Benjamin Franklin, contributed to discussions with his customary wit and moderating spirit. For the most part, the convention was a busy hive of politics as practiced by some of the new country's most educated and experienced young men: "The convention had been going seven hours a day, from 10 a.m. to 4 p.m., six days a week, for more than two full months. Each day the routine was the same. New Hampshire Delegate John Langdon, who finally arrived July 23, described it in a letter to a friend: 'The Great Washington, with a Dignity peculiar to himself, [takes] the Chair, the Notables are Seated, in a moment and after a short Silence, the Business of the day is opened, with great solemnity and good order.' Then would follow seven hours of declarations, declamations, animadversions and resolveds; the scratching sounds of quills on paper; occasionally someone raising his voice to make a point; others droning on in two- or three-hour disquisitions.

"At night and in the delegates' spare hours, the business continued unabated, for often the parties they held among themselves were mere extensions of the formal sessions at the State House. What they resolved in private, how many potential clauses were washed down with Madeira, no delegate ever chose to say, but there is evidence that this convention within the convention was used to limit the agenda, rather than expand it."[2]

In September, almost all of the convention delegates signed on—only three refused, including Edmund Randolph, but this dissent was a sign of the coming fierce campaign for the Constitution's establishment. By September 17, 1787, the delegates had, to everyone's wonder and yet to no one's complete satisfaction, completed the document that would, after its reception by the Continental Congress, bypass the state legislatures and go directly to special state conventions for ratification. If nine states voted for ratification, the Constitution would become law, though its success in four key states was regarded as essential for its successful application: Pennsylvania, Massachusetts, Virginia, and New York. The decision of whether or not to ratify the Constitution in state conventions by the citizens of the thirteen states, who were so recently survivors of a revolution, and accustomed to thinking of their hard-won fight as a guarantee of local government, meant giving up those ideals, those terms for which they had fought, for a new experiment: "In shifting power from the states, where new men dominated, to a new central government, the Constitution would reverse the verdict of 1776 on who would rule in America."[3] For the coming ten months, until Virginia's ratification on June 25, 1788, and New York's on July 26, there were fiery arguments and debates in all the states except Rhode Island, which ignored the convention and did not even ratify the Constitution until 1790. (North Carolina, the twelfth state, ratified the *fait accompli* in November of 1789.)

Many of the fears about and criticisms of aspects of the Constitution were, in their time, sensible and reasonable, and, even today, are still

---

[2] Fred Barbash. *The Founding: A Dramatic Account of the Writing of the Constitution.* New York: Simon and Schuster. 1987. 137.

[3] Isaac Kramnick. Introduction. *The Federalist Papers.* London: Penguin. 1987. 15.

being argued. One of the greatest, most important men in the Constitution's successful establishment, Alexander Hamilton, had himself
profound objections to it. On September 17, according to Madison's
notes, "Mr. Hamilton expressed his anxiety that every member should
sign. A few characters of consequence, by opposing, or even refusing
to sign the Constitution, might do infinite mischief by kindling the
latent sparks that lurk under an enthusiasm in favor of the convention,
which may soon subside. No man's ideas were more remote from the
plan than his own were known to be; but is it possible to deliberate between anarchy and convulsion on one side, and the chance of
good to be expected from the plan on the other?"[4] So Hamilton, with
James Madison and John Jay, in the magnificent *Federalist Papers*, an
anonymously authored team project of eighty-five essays published
in newspapers, argued for and explicated the Constitution before its
ratification by the voters of New York. Hamilton knew the document's
weaknesses and defended them, while proceeding with and extolling
its advantages. Madison seems to have had more faith in its ultimate
good, even while rueing several of its compromises. The authors of
The Federalist "recognized that, to a people only slowly emerging from
a deep depression, it would be essential to establish the prospect of a
proposed union as being essential to a revival of prosperity. Second, it
was necessary to demonstrate wherein the Articles of Confederation
had failed the nation."[5] These essays, only one of many series of arguments for or against the proposed Constitution, written of necessity
at speed, are lightning strikes of passionate intelligence, and contain
the arguments that have remained in large part the justifications for
and interpretations of the Constitution. As Madison wrote in a letter
to Thomas Jefferson years later, "The 'Federalist' may fairly enough be
regarded as the most authentic exposition of the text of the federal
Constitution, as understood by the Body which prepared & the Authority which accepted it. Yet it did not foresee all the misconstructions which have occurred; nor prevent some that it did foresee. And
what equally deserves remark, neither of the great rival Parties have
acquiesced in all its comments. It may nevertheless be admissible as a
School book . . ."[6]

   Whole-hearted and sincere criticisms of the Constitution, by great
American patriots, including Patrick Henry (two of whose ringing

---

[4] *The Records of the Federal Convention of 1787.* Edited by Max Farrand. Volume 2. New Ha-
ven: Yale University Press. 1911. Vol. 2. 645–646.

[5] Richard B. Morris. *Witnesses at the Creation: Hamilton, Madison, Jay and the Constitution.* New
York: Henry Holt. 1985. 15.

[6] James Madison to Thomas Jefferson. Letter of February 8, 1825.

speeches appear in this volume), have proved off-base, but the political process by which ratification came about and by which the Constitution was brought to completion, reflects our continued anxiety about where and how and when and why the United States government should operate. "Although the Constitution contains only about 6,000 words," a contemporary historian reminds us, "millions of additional words have been issued by the courts . . . in order to elucidate it."[7] That the Constitution failed in several ways, notably in regard to slavery, was obvious then, as now. The slave trade was an issue that made many of the makers, Enlightenment-educated thinkers, aware of their own hypocrisy in desiring liberty and self-government. To establish the Constitution, however, they compromised with the slaveholding and slave-dealing interests, and the moral hellhole they thus accepted would nearly destroy the country in the 1860s.

But the delegates to the Constitutional Convention got so much else right. There had never been such a well-knit, far-reaching, inclusive large government with such allowance for movement and incremental change. No one working sincerely at the Convention believed in an ideal government, so they made one that worked. Madison reminded readers of *The Federalist* that "If men were angels, no government would be necessary." The Constitution's practicality, its built-in system of checks and balances and corrections and amendments, has made it the hardiest, most long-lasting, most-admired national document in history. In 1878, the British prime minister William Gladstone remarked: "It is always interesting to trace and to compare Constitutions, as it is to compare languages . . . The two constitutions of the two countries express indeed rather the differences than the resemblances of the nations. The one is a thing grown, the other a thing made; the one a *praxis,* the other a *poiesis;* the one the offspring of tendency and indeterminate time, the other of choice and of an epoch. But, as the British Constitution is the most subtle organism which has proceeded from the womb and the long gestation of progressive history, so the American Constitution is, so far as I can see, the most wonderful work ever struck off at a given time by the brain and purpose of man."[8]

★ ★ ★

The documents and speeches in this compilation are an assortment of the most public and the most private and secret. There are several samplings from the notes of the speeches and debates within the Con-

---

[7] Michael G. Kammen. *A Machine That Would Go of Itself.* New York: Knopf. 1986. 12.
[8] William Ewart Gladstone. *Gleanings of Past Years: 1843–78.* Vol. 1. John Murray: London. 1879. 211-212.

stitutional Convention, recorded by Madison and published only after all the participants' deaths, on such topics as voting rights, the executive branch, and the slave trade. "On entering the field of debate on constitutional topics," wrote the nineteenth-century historian Jonathan Elliot, "an acquaintance with these opinions and sentiments must certainly be of the first importance ... In exercising the powers of legislation, could Congress consult higher authority? In expounding parts of the Constitution which seem extremely doubtful, the publication of the Proceedings and Debates of the states must, at least, be *useful*; for what the states really intended to grant to the general government must be looked for in their acts, and in their discussions, which manifest their *intentions*, in a manner peculiarly satisfactory, touching constitutional topics, so frequently the subject of controversy in Congress, and in the legal tribunals of the country."[9]

Among the other selections here are the more famous published proposals and legal documents submitted by the various groups, including the ultimately unsatisfactory Articles of Confederation, and, of course, the Constitution and its first ten amendments, the Bill of Rights. Also herein are a few of the private letters exchanged by the Founding Fathers regarding the defects, strengths, and necessity of this Constitution. Finally, there are several pieces chosen from among the thousands of essays and pamphlets rallying the Federalist and Anti-Federalist parties, notably those containing fundamental or passionate arguments for and against the Constitution.

The selections proceed chronologically, with brief introductory remarks, and it is hoped that all together the documents, debates, essays, and letters will suggest a narrative from which readers might make further research into the particular men, moments, and issues, and thereby discover and understand additional compelling stories illuminating the American miracle of the making of the Constitution.

—*Bob Blaisdell*

NOTE: The complete text of the U.S. Constitution begins on page 71 of the Dover edition.

---

[9] Jonathan Elliot. *The Debates in the Several State Conventions on the Adoption of the Federal Constitution, as Recommended by the General Convention at Philadelphia, in 1787*. Jonathan Lippincott: Philadelphia. 1888. Vol. I. iv.

THE UNITED STATES CONSTITUTION
DEBATES AND DOCUMENTS

CONTENTS

page

March 1, 1781: The Articles of Confederation (". . . the
Articles of this Confederation shall be inviolably observed
by every State, and the Union shall be perpetual . . .") 1

September 11–14, 1786; February 21, 1787: The Proceedings
and the Report of the Commissioners to Remedy Defects
of the Federal Government ("That there are important
defects in the system of the federal government is
acknowledged by the acts of all those states which have
concurred in the present meeting . . .") 10

March 31, 1787: Letter from George Washington to James
Madison (". . . my wish is, that the Convention may adopt
no temporizing expedient, but probe the defects of the
Constitution to the bottom, and provide radical cures . . .") 17

April 1787: Memoranda by James Madison: "Vices of the
Political System of the United States" ("The great
desideratum in government is such a modification of the
sovereignty as will render it sufficiently neutral between
the different interests and factions . . .") 21

May 28–29, 1787: Rules to Be Observed as the Standing
Orders of the Convention (". . . whilst [the president] shall
be speaking, none shall pass between them, or hold
discourse with another, or read a book, pamphlet, or paper,
printed or manuscript . . .") 30

May 29, 1787: The "Virginia Plan," Resolutions Offered by
    Edmund Randolph to the Federal Convention ("The
    Articles of the Confederation ought to be so corrected and
    enlarged as to accomplish the objects proposed by their
    institution . . .")   34
May 31, 1787: Debate in the Constitutional Convention on
    Suffrage: Elbridge Gerry, George Mason, James Wilson,
    James Madison, Edmund Randolph, and Others
    ("Mr. Wilson contended strenuously for drawing the most
    numerous branch of the legislature immediately from the
    people")   37
June 1 and June 4, 1787: Debate in the Constitutional
    Convention on Executive Power: Charles Pinckney, James
    Wilson, James Madison, and Others ("Mr. Madison
    thought it would be proper, before a choice should be
    made between a unity and a plurality in the executive,
    to fix the extent of the executive authority")   42
June 30, 1787: Debate in the Constitutional Convention on
    Small States Versus the Large States: Speech by Gunning
    Bedford, Jr., of Delaware (". . . the larger states proceed as
    if our eyes were already perfectly blinded")   51
August 21–22, 1787: Debate in the Constitutional
    Convention on the Slave Trade: Luther Martin, John
    Rutledge, George Mason, Charles Pinckney, and Others
    (". . . it was inconsistent with the principles of the
    revolution, and dishonorable to the American character, to
    have such a feature in the Constitution")   54
September 10, 1787: Debate on Amendments to the
    Constitution in the Federal Convention: Elbridge Gerry,
    Alexander Hamilton, James Madison, Edmund Randolph,
    and Others ("The national legislature will be the first to
    perceive and will be most sensible to the necessity of
    amendments, and ought also to be empowered whenever
    two thirds of each branch should concur to call a
    convention")   60
September 17, 1787: Address to the Constitutional
    Convention by Benjamin Franklin ("Thus I consent, sir,
    to this Constitution because I expect no better, and
    because I am not sure that it is not the best")   67

September 17, 1787: Letter of the President of the Federal
    Convention, George Washington, to the President of
    Congress, Transmitting the Constitution (". . . the
    Constitution, which we now present, is the result of a
    spirit of amity, and of that mutual deference and concession
    which the peculiarity of our political situation rendered
    indispensable")   69
September 17, 1787: The Constitution of the United States
    of America   71
October 1787: Notes: Objections to the Constitution by
    George Mason of Virginia ("This government will set out
    a moderate aristocracy: it is at present impossible to foresee
    whether it will, in its operation, produce a monarchy, or a
    corrupt tyrannical aristocracy")   83
October 5, 1787: Article, *Centinel* No. 1, "To the Freemen of
    Pennsylvania," by Samuel Bryan ("The constitution of
    Pennsylvania is yet in existence, as yet you have the right
    to freedom of speech and of publishing your sentiments")   86
November 22, 1787: Article, *The Federalist*, No. 10: "The
    Union as a Safeguard Against Domestic Faction and
    Insurrection," by James Madison (". . . the *causes* of faction
    cannot be removed, and . . . relief is only to be sought in
    the means of controlling its *effects*")   96
December 6, 1787: Letter by John Adams to Thomas Jefferson
    (". . . elections to offices which are great objects of
    ambition, I look at with terror")   103
December 20, 1787: Letter by Thomas Jefferson to James
    Madison (". . . a bill of rights is what the people are
    entitled to against every government on earth . . .")   105
January 25, 1788: Debate in the Massachusetts Ratifying
    Convention: Amos Singletary and Jonathan B. Smith
    (". . . I have known the worth of good government by the
    want of it")   110
February 5, 1788: Debate in the Massachusetts Ratifying
    Convention: Speech by Nathaniel Barrell (". . . excellent as
    this system is, in some respects it needs alterations . . .")   114
February 6, 1788: Article, *The Federalist*, No. 51, "The
    Structure of the Government Must Furnish the Proper
    Checks and Balances Between the Different Departments,"
    by James Madison ("If men were angels, no government
    would be necessary")   117

March–April 1788: Address to the People of the State of
   New York by John Jay, "A Citizen of New York" ("Suppose
   this plan to be rejected; what measures would you propose
   for obtaining a better?")   122
May 28, 1788: Article, *The Federalist*, No. 85, "Concluding
   Remarks," by Alexander Hamilton ("Let us now pause
   and ask ourselves whether . . . the proposed Constitution
   has not been satisfactorily vindicated from the aspersions
   thrown upon it")   132
June 4, 1788: On "Altering Our Federal Government":
   Speech by Patrick Henry of Virginia ("My political
   curiosity, exclusive of my anxious solicitude for the public
   welfare, leads me to ask, Who authorized them to speak
   the language of 'We, the people,' instead of 'We, the
   states'?")   139
June 24, 1788: Debate on the Absence of a Bill of Rights:
   James Madison and Patrick Henry (". . . I would declare it
   infinitely more safe, in its present form, than it would be
   after introducing into it that long train of alterations which
   they call amendments")   142
December 15, 1791: The Bill of Rights   153

The United States Constitution

The Full Text with
Supplementary Materials

THE ARTICLES OF CONFEDERATION

("... the Articles of this Confederation shall be inviolably observed
by every State, and the Union shall be perpetual ...")

MARCH 1, 1781

> *Hammered out in Philadelphia in July of 1776, the Articles of Con-*
> *federation were debated for more than a year before they were agreed*
> *to by the Continental Congress on November 15, 1777. The docu-*
> *ment was then sent to the state legislatures for approval; it required all*
> *thirteen states' approval for ratification, which came finally in 1781*
> *when Maryland signed on. The Revolutionary War ended in 1783,*
> *and in the next few years, the Congress of the Confederation's weak-*
> *nesses (see James Madison's "The Vices of the Political System of*
> *the United States" below) led to delegates from Virginia calling for*
> *a Federal Convention that would create a more effective and more*
> *centralized government.*

To all to whom these Presents shall come, we the undersigned Delegates of the States affixed to our Names send greeting.

Articles of Confederation and perpetual Union between the states of New Hampshire, Massachusetts-bay, Rhode Island and Providence Plantations, Connecticut, New York, New Jersey, Pennsylvania, Delaware, Maryland, Virginia, North Carolina, South Carolina and Georgia.

I.

The Stile of this Confederacy shall be "The United States of America."

II.

Each state retains its sovereignty, freedom, and independence, and every power, jurisdiction, and right, which is not by this Confederation expressly delegated to the United States, in Congress assembled.

III.

The said States hereby severally enter into a firm league of friendship with each other, for their common defense, the security of their liberties, and their mutual and general welfare, binding themselves to assist each other, against all force offered to, or attacks made upon them, or any of them, on account of religion, sovereignty, trade, or any other pretense whatever.

IV.

The better to secure and perpetuate mutual friendship and intercourse among the people of the different States in this Union, the free inhabitants of each of these States, paupers, vagabonds, and fugitives from justice excepted, shall be entitled to all privileges and immunities of free citizens in the several States; and the people of each State shall free ingress and regress to and from any other State, and shall enjoy therein all the privileges of trade and commerce, subject to the same duties, impositions, and restrictions as the inhabitants thereof respectively, provided that such restrictions shall not extend so far as to prevent the removal of property imported into any State, to any other State, of which the owner is an inhabitant; provided also that no imposition, duties or restriction shall be laid by any State, on the property of the United States, or either of them.

If any person guilty of, or charged with, treason, felony, or other high misdemeanor in any State, shall flee from justice, and be found in any of the United States, he shall, upon demand of the Governor or executive power of the State from which he fled, be delivered up and removed to the State having jurisdiction of his offense.

Full faith and credit shall be given in each of these States to the records, acts, and judicial proceedings of the courts and magistrates of every other State.

V.

For the most convenient management of the general interests of the United States, delegates shall be annually appointed in such manner as the legislatures of each State shall direct, to meet in Congress on the first Monday in November, in every year, with a power reserved to each State to recall its delegates, or any of them, at any time within the year, and to send others in their stead for the remainder of the year.

No State shall be represented in Congress by less than two, nor more than seven members; and no person shall be capable of being a delegate for more than three years in any term of six years; nor shall any person, being a delegate, be capable of holding any office under the United States, for which he, or another for his benefit, receives any salary, fees or emolument of any kind.

Each State shall maintain its own delegates in a meeting of the States, and while they act as members of the committee of the States.

In determining questions in the United States in Congress assembled, each State shall have one vote.

Freedom of speech and debate in Congress shall not be impeached or questioned in any court or place out of Congress, and the members of Congress shall be protected in their persons from arrests or imprisonments, during the time of their going to and from, and attendance on Congress, except for treason, felony, or breach of the peace.

VI.

No State, without the consent of the United States in Congress assembled, shall send any embassy to, or receive any embassy from, or enter into any conference, agreement, alliance or treaty with any King, Prince or State; nor shall any person holding any office of profit or trust under the United States, or any of them, accept any present, emolument, office or title of any kind whatever from any King, Prince or foreign State; nor shall the United States in Congress assembled, or any of them, grant any title of nobility.

No two or more States shall enter into any treaty, confederation or alliance whatever between them, without the consent of the United States in Congress assembled, specifying accurately the purposes for which the same is to be entered into, and how long it shall continue.

No State shall lay any imposts or duties, which may interfere with any stipulations in treaties, entered into by the United States in Congress assembled, with any King, Prince or State, in pursuance of any treaties already proposed by Congress, to the courts of France and Spain.

No vessel of war shall be kept up in time of peace by any State, except such number only, as shall be deemed necessary by the United States in Congress assembled, for the defense of such State, or its trade; nor shall any body of forces be kept up by any State in time of peace, except such number only, as in the judgement of the United States in Congress assembled, shall be deemed requisite to garrison the forts necessary for the defense of such State; but every State shall always keep up a well-regulated and disciplined militia, sufficiently armed and accoutered, and shall provide and constantly have ready for use, in public stores, a due number of filed pieces and tents, and a proper quantity of arms, ammunition and camp equipage.

No State shall engage in any war without the consent of the United States in Congress assembled, unless such State be actually invaded by enemies, or shall have received certain advice of a resolution being formed by some nation of Indians to invade such State, and the danger is so imminent as not to admit of a delay till the United States in Congress assembled can be consulted; nor shall any State grant commissions to any ships or vessels of war, nor letters of marque or reprisal, except it be after a declaration of war by the United States in Congress assembled, and then only against the Kingdom or State and the subjects thereof, against which war has been so declared, and under such regulations as shall be established by the United States in Congress assembled, unless such State be infested by pirates, in which case vessels of war may be fitted out for that occasion, and kept so long as the danger shall continue, or until the United States in Congress assembled shall determine otherwise.

VII.

When land forces are raised by any State for the common defense, all officers of or under the rank of colonel, shall be appointed by the legislature of each State respectively, by whom such forces shall be raised, or in such manner as such State shall direct, and all vacancies shall be filled up by the State which first made the appointment.

VIII.

All charges of war, and all other expenses that shall be incurred for the common defense or general welfare, and allowed by the United States in Congress assembled, shall be defrayed out of a common treasury, which shall be supplied by the several States in proportion to the value of all land within each State, granted or surveyed for any person, as such land and the buildings and improvements thereon shall be estimated according to such mode as the United States in Congress assembled, shall from time to time direct and appoint.

The taxes for paying that proportion shall be laid and levied by the authority and direction of the legislatures of the several States within the time agreed upon by the United States in Congress assembled.

IX.

The United States in Congress assembled, shall have the sole and exclusive right and power of determining on peace and war, except in the cases mentioned in the sixth article — of sending and receiving ambassadors — entering into treaties and alliances, provided that no treaty of commerce shall be made whereby the legislative power of the respective States shall be restrained from imposing such imposts and duties on foreigners, as their own people are subjected to, or from prohibiting the exportation or importation of any species of goods or commodities whatsoever—of establishing rules for deciding in all cases, what captures on land or water shall be legal, and in what manner prizes taken by land or naval forces in the service of the United States shall be divided or appropriated—of granting letters of marque and reprisal in times of peace—appointing courts for the trial of piracies and felonies committed on the high seas and establishing courts for receiving and determining finally appeals in all cases of captures, provided that no member of Congress shall be appointed a judge of any of the said courts.

The United States in Congress assembled shall also be the last resort on appeal in all disputes and differences now subsisting or that hereafter may arise between two or more States concerning boundary, jurisdiction or any other causes whatever; which authority shall always be exercised in the manner following. Whenever the legislative or executive authority or lawful agent of any State in controversy with another shall present a petition to Congress stating the matter in question and praying for a hearing, notice thereof shall be given by order of Congress to the legislative or executive authority of the other State in controversy, and a day assigned for the appearance of the parties by their lawful agents, who shall then be directed to appoint by joint consent, commissioners or judges to constitute a court for hearing and determining the matter in question: but if they cannot agree, Congress shall name three persons out of each of the United States, and from the list of such persons each party shall alternately strike out one, the petitioners beginning, until the number shall be reduced to thirteen; and from that number not less than seven, nor more than nine names as Congress shall direct, shall in the presence of Congress be drawn out by lot, and the persons whose names shall be so drawn or any five of them, shall be commissioners or judges, to hear and finally determine the controversy, so always as a major part of the judges who shall hear the cause shall agree in the determination: and if either party shall neglect to attend at the day appointed, without showing reasons, which Congress shall judge sufficient, or being present shall refuse to strike, the Congress shall proceed to nominate three persons out of each State, and the secretary of Congress shall strike in behalf of such party absent or refusing; and the judgement and sentence of the court to be appointed, in the manner before prescribed, shall be final and conclusive; and if any of the parties shall refuse to submit to the authority of such court, or to appear or defend their claim or cause, the court shall nevertheless proceed to pronounce sentence, or judgement, which shall in like manner be final and decisive, the judgement or sentence and other proceedings being in either case transmitted to Congress, and lodged among the acts of Congress for the security of the parties concerned: provided that every commissioner, before he sits in judgement, shall take an oath to be administered by one of the judges of the supreme or superior court of the State, where the cause shall be tried, "well and truly to hear and determine the matter in question, according to the best of his judgement, without favor, affection or hope of reward": provided also, that no State shall be deprived of territory for the benefit of the United States.

All controversies concerning the private right of soil claimed under different grants of two or more States, whose jurisdictions as they may respect such lands, and the States which passed such grants are adjusted, the said grants or either of them being at the same time claimed to have originated antecedent to such settlement of jurisdiction, shall on the petition of either party to the Congress of the United States, be finally determined as near as may be in the same manner as is before prescribed for deciding disputes respecting territorial jurisdiction between different States.

The United States in Congress assembled shall also have the sole and exclusive right and power of regulating the alloy and value of coin struck by their own authority, or by that of the respective States—fixing the standards of weights and measures throughout the United States—regulating the trade and managing all affairs with the Indians, not members of any of the States, provided that the legislative right of any State within its own limits be not infringed or violated—establishing or regulating post offices from one State to another, throughout all the United States, and exacting such postage on the papers passing through the same as may be requisite to defray the expenses of the said office—appointing all officers of the land forces, in the service of the United States, excepting regimental officers—appointing all the officers of the naval forces, and commissioning all officers whatever in the service of the United States—making rules for the government and regulation of the said land and naval forces, and directing their operations.

The United States in Congress assembled shall have authority to appoint a committee, to sit in the recess of Congress, to be denominated "A Committee of the States," and to consist of one delegate from each State; and to appoint such other committees and civil officers as may be necessary for managing the general affairs of the United States under their direction—to appoint one of their members to preside, provided that no person be allowed to serve in the office of president more than one year in any term of three years; to ascertain the necessary sums of money to be raised for the service of the United States, and to appropriate and apply the same for defraying the public expenses—to borrow money, or emit bills on the credit of the United States, transmitting every half-year to the respective States an account of the sums of money so borrowed or emitted—to build and equip a navy—to agree upon the number of land forces, and to make requisitions from each State for its quota, in proportion to the number of white inhabitants in such State; which requisition shall be binding, and thereupon the legislature of each State shall appoint the regimental officers, raise the men and clothe, arm and equip them in a solid-like manner, at the expense of the United States; and the officers and men so clothed, armed and equipped shall march to the place appointed, and within the time agreed on by the United States in Congress assembled. But if the United States in Congress assembled shall, on consideration of circumstances judge proper that any State should not raise men, or should raise a smaller number of men than the quota thereof, such extra number shall be raised, officered, clothed, armed and equipped in the same manner as the quota of each State, unless the legislature of such State shall judge that such extra number cannot be safely spread out in the same, in which case they shall raise, officer, clothe, arm and equip as many of such extra number as they judge can be safely spared. And the officers and men so clothed, armed, and equipped, shall march to the place appointed, and within the time agreed on by the United States in Congress assembled.

The United States in Congress assembled shall never engage in a war, nor grant letters of marque or reprisal in time of peace, nor enter into any treaties or alliances, nor coin money, nor regulate the value thereof, nor ascertain the sums and expenses necessary for the defense and welfare of the United States, or any of them, nor emit bills, nor borrow money on the credit of the United States, nor appropriate money, nor agree upon the number of vessels of war, to be built or purchased, or the number of land or sea forces to be raised, nor appoint a commander in chief of the army or navy, unless nine States assent to the same: nor shall a question on any other point, except for adjourning from day to day be determined, unless by the votes of the majority of the United States in Congress assembled.

The Congress of the United States shall have power to adjourn to any time within the year, and to any place within the United States, so that no period of adjournment be for a longer duration than the space of six months, and shall publish the journal of their proceedings monthly, except such parts thereof relating to treaties, alliances or military operations, as in their judgement require secrecy; and the yeas and nays of the delegates of each State on any question shall be entered on the journal, when it is desired by any delegates of a State, or any of them, at his or their request shall be furnished with a transcript of the said journal, except such parts as are above excepted, to lay before the legislatures of the several States.

X.

The Committee of the States, or any nine of them, shall be authorized to execute, in the recess of Congress, such of the powers of Congress as the United States in Congress assembled, by the consent of the nine States, shall from time to time think expedient to vest them with; provided that no power be delegated to the said Committee, for the exercise of which, by the Articles of Confederation, the voice of nine States in the Congress of the United States assembled be requisite.

XI.

Canada acceding to this confederation, and adjoining in the measures of the United States, shall be admitted into, and entitled to all the advantages of this Union; but no other colony shall be admitted into the same, unless such admission be agreed to by nine States.

XII.

All bills of credit emitted, monies borrowed, and debts contracted by, or under the authority of Congress, before the assembling of the United States, in pursuance of the present confederation, shall be deemed and considered as a charge against the United States, for payment and satisfaction whereof the said United States, and the public faith are hereby solemnly pledged.

XIII.

Every State shall abide by the determination of the United States in Congress assembled, on all questions which by this confederation are submitted to them. And the Articles of this Confederation shall be inviolably observed by every State, and the Union shall be perpetual; nor shall any alteration at any time hereafter be made in any of them; unless such alteration be agreed to in a Congress of the United States, and be afterwards confirmed by the legislatures of every State.

And Whereas it hath pleased the Great Governor of the World to incline the hearts of the legislatures we respectively represent in Congress, to approve of, and to authorize us to ratify the said Articles of Confederation and perpetual Union. Know Ye that we the undersigned delegates, by virtue of the power and authority to us given for that purpose, do by these presents, in the name and in behalf of our respective constituents, fully and entirely ratify and confirm each and every of the said Articles of Confederation and perpetual Union, and all and singular the matters and things therein contained: And we do further solemnly plight and engage the faith of our respective constituents, that they shall abide by the determinations of the United States in Congress assembled, on all questions, which by the said Confederation are submitted to them. And that the Articles thereof shall be inviolably observed by the States we respectively represent, and that the Union shall be perpetual.

In Witness whereof we have hereunto set our hands in Congress. Done at Philadelphia in the State of Pennsylvania the ninth day of July in the Year of our Lord One Thousand Seven Hundred and Seventy-Eight, and in the Third Year of the independence of America.

Agreed to by Congress 15 November 1777. In force after ratification by Maryland, 1 March 1781.

THE PROCEEDINGS AND THE REPORT OF THE COMMISSIONERS TO REMEDY DEFECTS OF THE FEDERAL GOVERNMENT

("That there are important defects in the system of the federal government is acknowledged by the acts of all those states which have concurred in the present meeting ...")

SEPTEMBER 11–14, 1786
FEBRUARY 21, 1787

To begin taking steps toward a federal constitution, the Virginia House of Delegates' General Assembly proposed on January 21, 1786, to appoint eight commissioners (among them James Madison, Edmund Randolph, and George Mason) to meet with commissioners from other states "to take into consideration the trade of the United States; to examine the relative situation and trade of the said states; to consider how far a uniform system in their commercial regulations may be necessary to their common interest and their permanent harmony; and to report to the several states such an act relative to this great object as, when unanimously ratified by them, will enable the United States in Congress assembled effectually to provide for the same." In July 1786, Governor Patrick Henry signed off on the proposition, and in mid-September 1786, commissioners from five states met in Annapolis, Maryland. While as a small body they were unable to rectify any defects in national governance and trade, the important outcome of the meeting was the call for the next spring's Federal (or Constitutional) Convention in Philadelphia.

Annapolis, in the State of Maryland, September 11, 1786.—At a meeting of commissioners from the states of New York, New Jersey, Pennsylvania, Delaware, and Virginia:

PRESENT,

New York.	Delaware.
Alexander Hamilton,	George Read,
Egbert Benson.	John Dickinson,
	Richard Bassett.
New Jersey.	Virginia.
Abraham Clark,	Edmund Randolph,
William C Houston,	James Madison, Jun.,
James Schureman.	St. George Tucker.
Pennsylvania.	
Tench Coxe.	

Mr. Dickinson was unanimously elected chairman.

The commissioners produced their credentials from their respective states, which were read.

After a full communication of sentiments, and deliberate consideration of what would be proper to be done by the commissioners now assembled, it was unanimously agreed that a committee be appointed to prepare a draft of a report to be made to the states having commissioners attending at this meeting.

Adjourned till Wednesday morning.

Wednesday, September 13, 1786.—Met agreeably to adjournment.

The committee appointed for that purpose reported the draft of the report, which being read, the meeting proceeded to the consideration thereof; and, after some time spent therein, adjourned till tomorrow morning.

Thursday, September 14, 1786.—Met agreeably to adjournment.

The meeting resumed the consideration of the draft of the report, and, after some time spent therein, and amendments made, the same was unanimously agreed to, and is as follows, to wit:—

> To the Honorable the Legislatures of Virginia, Delaware, Pennsylvania, New Jersey, and New York, the commissioners from the said states respectively, assembled at Annapolis, humbly beg leave to report,—
>
> That, pursuant to their several appointments, they met at Annapolis in the state of Maryland, on the 11th day of September instant; and having proceeded to a communication of their powers, they found that the states of New York, Pennsylvania, and Virginia, had, in substance, and nearly in the same terms, authorized their respective commissioners "to meet such commissioners as were or might be appointed by the

other states in the Union, at such time and place as should
be agreed upon by the said commissioners, to take into consideration the trade and commerce of the United States; to
consider how far a uniform system in their commercial intercourse and regulations might be necessary to their common
interest and permanent harmony; and to report to the several
states such an act relative to this great object as, when unanimously ratified by them, would enable the United States in
Congress assembled effectually to provide for the same."

That the state of Delaware had given similar powers to
their commissioners, with this difference only, that the act to
be framed in virtue of these powers is required to be reported
"to the United States in Congress assembled, to be agreed to
by them, and confirmed by the legislatures of every state."

That the state of New Jersey had enlarged the object of their
appointment, empowering their commissioners "to consider
how far a uniform system in their commercial regulations and
other important matters might be necessary to the common
interest and permanent harmony of the several states;" and to
report such an act on the subject as, when ratified by them,
"would enable the United States in Congress assembled effectually to provide for the exigencies of the Union."

That appointments of commissioners have also been made
by the states of New Hampshire, Massachusetts, Rhode Island,
and North Carolina, none of whom, however, have attended;
but that no information has been received, by your commissioners, of any appointment having been made by the states of
Connecticut, Maryland, South Carolina, or Georgia.

That the express terms of the powers to your commissioners supposing a deputation from all the states, and having for
object the trade and commerce of the United States, your
commissioners did not conceive it advisable to proceed on
the business of their mission under the circumstance of so
partial and defective a representation.

Deeply impressed, however, with the magnitude and importance of the object confided to them on this occasion,
your commissioners cannot forbear to indulge an expression
of their earnest and unanimous wish, that speedy measures
may be taken to effect a general meeting of the states, in a future convention, for the same and such other purposes as the
situation of public affairs may be found to require.

If, in expressing this wish, or in intimating any other
sentiment, your commissioners should seem to exceed the

strict bounds of their appointment, they entertain a full confidence that a conduct dictated by an anxiety for the welfare of the United States will not fail to receive an indulgent construction.

In this persuasion your commissioners submit an opinion, that the idea of extending the powers of their deputies to other objects than those of commerce, which has been adopted by the state of New Jersey, was an improvement on the original plan, and will deserve to be incorporated into that of a future convention. They are the more naturally led to this conclusion, as, in the course of their reflections on the subject, they have been induced to think that the power of regulating trade is of such comprehensive extent, and will enter so far into the general system of the federal government, that, to give it efficacy, and to obviate questions and doubts concerning its precise nature and limits, may require a correspondent adjustment of other parts of the federal system.

That there are important defects in the system of the federal government is acknowledged by the acts of all those states which have concurred in the present meeting; that the defects, upon a closer examination, may be found greater and more numerous than even these acts imply, is at least so far probable, from the embarrassments which characterize the present state of our national affairs, foreign and domestic, as may reasonably be supposed to merit a deliberate and candid discussion, in some mode which will unite the sentiments and councils of all the states. In the choice of the mode, your commissioners are of opinion that a convention of deputies from the different states, for the special and sole purpose of entering into this investigation, and digesting a plan for supplying such defects as may be discovered to exist, will be entitled to a preference, from considerations which will occur without being particularized.

Your commissioners decline an enumeration of those national circumstances on which their opinion respecting the propriety of a future convention, with more enlarged powers, is founded; as it would be a useless intrusion of facts and observations, most of which have been frequently the subject of public discussion, and none of which can have escaped the penetration of those to whom they would in this instance be addressed. They are, however, of a nature so serious, as, in the view of your commissioners, to render the situation of the United States delicate and critical, calling for an exertion of the united virtue and wisdom of all the members of the confederacy.

Under this impression, your commissioners, with the most respectful deference, beg leave to suggest their unanimous conviction, that it may essentially tend to advance the interests of the Union, if the states, by whom they have been respectively delegated, would themselves concur, and use their endeavors to procure the concurrence of the other states, in the appointment of commissioners, to meet at Philadelphia on the second Monday in May next, to take into consideration the situation of the United States, to devise such further provisions as shall appear to them necessary to render the constitution of the federal government adequate to the exigencies of the Union; and to report such an act for that purpose to the United States in Congress assembled, as, when agreed to by them, and afterwards confirmed by the legislatures of every state, will effectually provide for the same.

Though your commissioners could not with propriety address these observations and sentiments to any but the states they have the honor to represent, they have nevertheless concluded, from motives of respect, to transmit copies of this report to the United States in Congress assembled, and to the executive of the other states.

By order of the Commissioners.

Dated at Annapolis, September 14, 1786.

Resolved, That the chairman sign the aforegoing report in behalf of the commissioners. Then adjourned without day.

REPORT OF PROCEEDINGS

In Congress, Wednesday, February 21, 1787.

The report of a grand committee, consisting of Mr. Dane, Mr. Varnum, Mr. S. M. Mitchell, Mr. Smith, Mr. Cadwallader, Mr. Irvine, Mr. N. Mitchell, Mr. Forrest, Mr. Grayson, Mr. Blount, Mr. Bull, and Mr. Few, to whom was referred a letter of 14th September, 1786, from J. Dickinson, written at the request of commissioners from the states of Virginia, Delaware, Pennsylvania, New Jersey, and New York, assembled at the city of Annapolis, together with a copy of the report of the said commissioners to the legislatures of the states by whom they were appointed, being an order of the day, was called up, and which is contained in the following resolution, viz.:—

"Congress having had under consideration the letter of John Dickinson, Esq., chairman of the commissioners who assembled at Annapolis during the last year; also the proceedings of the said commissioners; and entirely coinciding with them as to the inefficiency of the federal government, and the necessity of devising such further provisions as shall render the same adequate to the exigencies of the Union, do strongly recommend to the different legislatures to send forward delegates, to meet the proposed convention, on the second Monday in May next, at the city of Philadelphia."

The delegates for the state of New York thereupon laid before Congress instructions which they had received from their constituents, and, in pursuance of the said instructions, moved to postpone the further consideration of the report in order to take up the following proposition, viz.:—

"That it be recommended to the states composing the Union, that a convention of representatives, from the said states respectively, be held at _____, on _____, for the purpose of revising the Articles of Confederation and Perpetual Union between the United States of America, and reporting to the United States in Congress assembled, and to the states respectively, such alterations and amendments of the said Articles of Confederation as the representatives met in such convention shall judge proper and necessary to render them adequate to the preservation and support of the Union."

On the question to postpone, for the purpose above mentioned, the yeas and nays being required by the delegates for New York:

Massachusetts,	Mr. King,	Ay. }	Ay.
	Mr. Dane,	Ay. }	
Connecticut,	Mr. Johnson,	Ay. }	Divided.
	Mr. S. Mitchell,	No. }	
New York,	Mr. Smith,	Ay. }	Ay.
	Mr. Benson,	Ay. }	
New Jersey,	Mr. Cadwallader,	Ay. }	
	Mr. Clark,	No. }	No.
	Mr. Schureman,	No. }	
Pennsylvania,	Mr. Irvine,	No. }	
	Mr. Meredith,	Ay. }	No. }
	Mr. Bingham,	No. }	

Delaware,	Mr. N Mitchell,	No.	
Maryland,	Mr. Forrest,	No.	
Virginia,	Mr. Grayson,	Ay. }	
	Mr. Madison,	Ay. }	Ay.
North Carolina,	Mr. Blount,	No. }	
	Mr. Hawkins,	No. }	No.
South Carolina,	Mr. Bull,	No. }	
	Mr. Kean,	No. }	
	Mr. Huger,	No. }	No.
	Mr. Parker,	No. }	
Georgia,	Mr. Few,	Ay. }	
	Mr. Pierce,	No. }	Divided.

So the question was lost.

A motion was then made, by the delegates for Massachusetts, to postpone the further consideration of the report, in order to take into consideration a motion which they read in their place. This being agreed to, the motion of the delegates for Massachusetts was taken up, and, being amended, was agreed to, as follows:—

"Whereas there is provision, in the Articles of Confederation and Perpetual Union, for making alterations therein, by the assent of a Congress of the United States, and of the legislatures of the several states; and whereas experience hath evinced that there are defects in the present Confederation; as a mean to remedy which, several of the states, and particularly the state of New York, by express instructions to their delegates in Congress, have suggested a convention for the purposes expressed in the following resolution: and such convention appearing to be the most probable mean of establishing in these states a firm national government,—

"*Resolved*, That, in the opinion of Congress, it is expedient that, on the second Monday in May next, a convention of delegates, who shall have been appointed by the several states, be held at Philadelphia, for the sole and express purpose of revising the Articles of Confederation, and reporting to Congress and the several legislatures such alterations and provisions therein as shall, when agreed to in Congress, and confirmed by the states, render the federal Constitution adequate to the exigencies of government and the preservation of the Union."

LETTER FROM GEORGE WASHINGTON TO JAMES MADISON

("... my wish is, that the Convention may adopt no temporizing
expedient, but probe the defects of the Constitution
to the bottom, and provide radical cures ...")

Mount Vernon, Virginia
March 31, 1787

*Though not at this time a politician, General Washington (1732–
1799), the national hero for his successful leadership of the Continental Army in the Revolutionary War, was as adamant as any about
the need for a new kind of government. Writing in the fall of 1786
to James Madison, the Virginia state legislator who was preparing
his plans for the Federal Constitutional Convention, he declared:
"Without an alteration in our political creed, the superstructure we
have been seven years in raising, at the expense of so much treasure
and blood, must fall. We are fast verging to anarchy and confusion.
Thirteen sovereignties pulling against each other, and all tugging at
the Federal head, will soon bring ruin on the whole; whereas a liberal
and energetic constitution, well checked and well watched to prevent
encroachments, might restore us to that degree of respectability and
consequence to which we had the fairest chance of attaining." The following letter, anticipating the Constitutional Convention, over which
Washington would preside (for the most part silently), suggests Washington's more specific wishes.*

My Dear Sir: At the same time that I acknowledge the receipt of
your obliging favor of the 21ˢᵗ ultimate from New York I promise to
avail myself of your indulgence of writing only when it is convenient
to me. If this should not occasion a relaxation on your part, I shall
become very much your debtor, and possibly like others in similar
circumstances (when the debt is burthensome) may feel a disposition
to apply the sponge, or, what is nearly akin to it, pay you off in depre-

ciated paper, which being a legal tender, or what is tantamount, being *that* or *nothing*, you cannot refuse. You will receive the nominal value, and that you know quiets the conscience, and makes all things easy, with the debtor.

I am glad to find that Congress have recommended to the states to appear in the convention proposed to be holden in Philadelphia in May. I think the reasons in favor, have the preponderancy of those against the measure. It is idle in my opinion to suppose that the Sovereign can be insensible of the inadequacy of the powers under which it acts, and that seeing, it should not recommend a revision of the federal system when it is considered by many as the *only* constitutional mode by which the defects can be remedied. Had Congress proceeded to a delineation of the powers, it might have sounded an alarm; but as the case is, I do not conceive that it will have that effect.

From the acknowledged abilities of the Secretary for Foreign Affairs [John Jay], I could have had no doubt of his having ably investigated the infractions of the Treaty [of Paris] on both sides. Much is it to be regretted however, that there should have been any on ours. We seem to have forgotten, or never to have learnt, the policy of placing one's enemy in the wrong. Had we observed good faith on our part, we might have told our tale to the world with a good grace; but complaints illy become those who are found to be the first aggressors.

I am fully of opinion that those who lean to a monarchial government have either not consulted the public mind, or that they live in a region where the leveling principles in which they were bred, being entirely eradicated, is much more productive of monarchical ideas than are to be found in the Southern states, where, from the habitual distinctions which have always existed among the people, one would have expected the first generation, and the most rapid growth of them. I also am clear, that even admitting the utility — nay, necessity — of the form, yet that the period is not arrived for adopting the change without shaking the peace of this country to its foundation.

That a thorough reform of the present system is indispensable, none who have capacities to judge will deny; and with hand (and heart) I hope the business will be essayed in a full convention. After which, if more powers, and more decision is not found in the existing form. If it still wants energy and that secrecy and dispatch (either from the nonattendance, or the local views of its members) which is characteristic of good government. And if it shall be found (the contrary of which however I have always been more afraid of, than of the abuse of them) that Congress will upon all proper occasions exercise the powers with a firm and steady hand, instead of frittering them back to the individual states, where the members in place of viewing themselves in their national character, are too apt to be looking. I say after this essay is made if the system proves inefficient, conviction of the necessity of a change will be disseminated among all classes of the people. Then, and not till then, in my opinion can it be attempted without involving all the evils of civil discord.

I confess however that my opinion of public virtue is so far changed that I have my doubts whether any system without the means of coercion in the sovereign, will enforce obedience to the ordinances of a general government; without which, everything else fails. Laws or ordinances unobserved, or partially attended to, had better never have been made; because the first is a mere nihil, and the second is productive of much jealousy and discontent. But the kind of coercion you may ask? This indeed will require thought; though the non-compliance of the states with the late requisition, is an evidence of the necessity. It is somewhat singular that a state (New York) which used to be foremost in all federal measures, should now turn her face against them in almost every instance.

I fear the state of Massachusetts have exceeded the bounds of good policy in its disfranchisements; punishment is certainly due to the disturbers of a government, but the operations of this act is too extensive. It embraces too much, and probably may give birth to new instead of destroying the old leven. Some acts passed at the last session of our assembly respecting the trade of this country, has given great, and general discontent to the merchants of it. An application from the whole body of those at Norfolk has been made, I am told, to convene the assembly.

I had written thus far, and was on the point of telling you how much I am your obliged servant, when your favor of the 18th calls upon me for additional acknowledgments. I thank you for the Indian vocabulary which I dare say will be very acceptable in a general comparison. Having taken a copy, I return you the original with thanks.

It gives me great pleasure to hear that there is a probability of a full representation of the states in Convention; but if the delegates come to it under fetters, the salutary ends proposed will in my opinion be greatly embarrassed and retarded, if not altogether defeated. I am anxious to know how this matter really is, as my wish is, that the Convention may adopt no temporizing expedient, but probe the defects of the Constitution to the bottom, and provide radical cures; whether they are agreed to or not; a conduct like this, will stamp wisdom and dignity on the proceedings, and be looked to as a luminary, which sooner or later will shed its influence.

I should feel pleasure, I confess, in hearing that Vermont is received into the Union upon terms agreeable to all parties.[1] I took the liberty years ago to tell some of the first characters in the state of New York, that sooner or later it would come to that. That the longer it was delayed the terms on their part, would, probably be more difficult; and that the general interest was suffering by the suspense in which the business was held; as the asylum which it afforded was a constant drain from the Army in place of an aid which it offered to afford. and lastly, considering the proximity of it to Canada if they were not with us, they might become a sore thorn in our sides, which I verily believe would have been the case if the war had continued. The Western settlements, without good and wise management of them, may be equally troublesome.

With sentiments of the sincerest friendship etc. Be so good as to forward the enclosed. Mrs. Washington intended to have sent it by Colonel Carrington, but he did not call here.

---

[1] Vermont became the fourteenth state in 1791.

MEMORANDA BY JAMES MADISON: "VICES OF THE POLITICAL SYSTEM OF THE UNITED STATES"

("The great desideratum in government is such a modification
of the sovereignty as will render it sufficiently neutral
between the different interests and factions . . .")

APRIL 1787

On account of his penetrating analysis here and elsewhere of the defects of the Articles of Confederation, his drafting of the Virginia Plan, his theories of political science and shrewd compromises at the Federal Convention, his authorship of many of the Federalist *Papers, and finally his agile defense of the Constitution at Virginia's Ratifying Convention in June 1788, James Madison (1751–1836) is justifiably regarded as "The Father of the Constitution." He became the fourth President of the United States in 1809.*

1. Failure of the States to comply with the Constitutional requisitions.
    This evil has been so fully experienced both during the war and since the peace, results so naturally from the number and independent authority of the States and has been so uniformly exemplified in every similar Confederacy, that it may be considered as not less radically and permanently inherent in, than it is fatal to the object of, the present system.
2. Encroachments by the States on the federal authority.
    Examples of this are numerous and repetitions may be foreseen in almost every case where any favorite object of a State shall present a temptation. Among these examples are the wars and Treaties of Georgia with the Indians—the unlicensed compacts between Virginia and Maryland, and between Pennsylvania and New Jersey—the troops raised and to be kept up by Massachusetts.

21

3. Violations of the law of nations and of treaties.

From the number of legislatures, the sphere of life from which most of their members are taken, and the circumstances under which their legislative business is carried on, irregularities of this kind must frequently happen. Accordingly not a year has passed without instances of them in some one or other of the States. The treaty of peace—the treaty with France—the treaty with Holland have each been violated. The causes of these irregularities must necessarily produce frequent violations of the law of nations in other respects.

As yet foreign powers have not been rigorous in animadverting on us. This moderation however cannot be mistaken for a permanent partiality to our faults, or a permanent security against those disputes with other nations, which being among the greatest of public calamities, it ought to be least in the power of any part of the community to bring on the whole.

4. Trespasses of the States on the rights of each other.

These are alarming symptoms, and may be daily apprehended as we are admonished by daily experience. See the law of Virginia restricting foreign vessels to certain ports—of Maryland in favor of vessels belonging to her own citizens—of New York in favor of the same.

Paper money, installments of debts, occlusion of courts, making property a legal tender, may likewise be deemed aggressions on the rights of other States. As the citizens of every State aggregately taken stand more or less in the relation of creditors or debtors, to the citizens of every other States, acts of the debtor State in favor of debtors, affect the creditor State, in the same manner, as they do its own citizens who are relatively creditors towards other citizens. This remark may be extended to foreign nations. If the exclusive regulation of the value and alloy of coin was properly delegated to the federal authority, the policy of it equally requires a control on the States in the cases above mentioned. It must have been meant

1. to preserve uniformity in the circulating medium throughout the nation.

2. to prevent those frauds on the citizens of other States, and the subjects of foreign powers, which might disturb the tranquility at home, or involve the Union in foreign contests.

The practice of many States in restricting the commercial intercourse with other States, and putting their productions and manufactures on the same footing with those of foreign nations, though not contrary to the federal articles, is certainly adverse to the spirit of the Union, and tends to beget retaliating regulations, not less expensive and vexatious in themselves, than they are destructive of the general harmony.

5. Want of concert in matters where common interest requires it.

This defect is strongly illustrated in the state of our commercial affairs. How much has the national dignity, interest, and revenue suffered from this cause? Instances of inferior moment are the want of uniformity in the laws concerning naturalization and literary property; of provision for national seminaries, for grants of incorporation for national purposes, for canals and other works of general utility, which may at present be defeated by the perverseness of particular States whose concurrence is necessary.

6. Want of guaranty to the States of their Constitutions and laws against internal violence.

The confederation is silent on this point and therefore by the second article the hands of the federal authority are tied. According to republican theory, right and power being both vested in the majority, are held to be synonymous. According to fact and experience a minority may in an appeal to force, be an overmatch for the majority.

1. If the minority happen to include all such as possess the skill and habits of military life, and such as possess the great pecuniary resources, one third only may conquer the remaining two thirds.

2. One third of those who participate in the choice of the rulers, may be rendered a majority by the accession of those whose poverty excludes them from a right of suffrage, and who for obvious reasons will be more likely to join the standard of sedition than that of the established government.

3. Where slavery exists the republican theory becomes still more fallacious.

7. Want of sanction to the laws, and of coercion in the Government of the Confederacy.

A sanction is essential to the idea of law, as coercion is to that of government. The federal system being destitute of both, wants the great vital principles of a political constitution. Under the form of such a constitution, it is in fact nothing more than a treaty of amity of commerce and of alliance, between so many independent and sovereign States. From what cause could so fatal an omission have happened in the Articles of Confederation? From a mistaken confidence that the justice, the good faith, the honor, the sound policy, of the several legislative assemblies would render superfluous any appeal to the ordinary motives by which the laws secure the obedience of individuals: a confidence which does honor to the enthusiastic virtue of the compilers, as much as the inexperience of the crisis apologizes for their errors. The time which has since elapsed has had the double effect, of increasing the light, and tempering the warmth, with which the arduous work may be revised. It is no longer doubted that a unanimous and punctual obedience of 13 independent bodies, to the acts of the federal government, ought not be calculated on. Even during the war, when external danger supplied in some degree the defect of legal and coercive sanctions, how imperfectly did the States fulfill their obligations to the Union? In time of peace, we see already what is to be expected. How indeed could it be otherwise?

In the first place, every general act of the Union must necessarily bear unequally hard on some particular member or members of it.

Secondly, the partiality of the members to their own interests and rights, a partiality which will be fostered by the courtiers of popularity, will naturally exaggerate the inequality where it exists, and even suspect it where it has no existence.

Thirdly, a distrust of the voluntary compliance of each other may prevent the compliance of any, although it should be the latent disposition of all. Here are causes and pretexts which will never fail to render federal measures abortive. If the laws of the States were merely recommendatory to their citizens, or if they were to be rejudged by county authorities, what security, what probability would exist, that they would be carried into execution? Is the security or probability greater in favor of the acts of Congress which depending for their execution on the will of the state legislatures, which are though nominally authoritative, in fact recommendatory only.

8. Want of ratification by the people of the Articles of Confederation.

In some of the States the Confederation is recognized by, and forms a part of, the Constitution. In others however it has received no other sanction than that of the legislative authority. From this defect two evils result:

1. Whenever a law of a State happens to be repugnant to an act of Congress, particularly when the latter is of posterior date to the former, it will be at least questionable whether the

latter must not prevail; and as the question must be decided by the Tribunals of the State, they will be most likely to lean on the side of the State.

2. As far as the Union of the States is to be regarded as a league of sovereign powers, and not as a political constitution by virtue of which they are become one sovereign power, so far it seems to follow from the doctrine of compacts, that a breach of any of the articles of the confederation by any of the parties to it, absolves the other parties from their respective obligations, and gives them a right if they choose to exert it, of dissolving the Union altogether.

9. Multiplicity of laws in the several States.

In developing the evils which vitiate the political system of the U.S., it is proper to include those which are found within the States individually, as well as those which directly affect the States collectively, since the former class have an indirect influence on the general malady and must not be overlooked in forming a complete remedy. Among the evils then of our situation may well be ranked the multiplicity of laws from which no State is exempt. As far as laws are necessary, to mark with precision the duties of those who are to obey them, and to take from those who are to administer them a discretion, which might be abused, their number is the price of liberty. As far as the laws exceed this limit, they are a nuisance: a nuisance of the most pestilent kind. Try the codes of the several States by this test, and what a luxuriancy of legislation do they present. The short period of independency has filled as many pages as the century which preceded it. Every year, almost every session, adds a new volume. This may be the effect in part, but it can only be in part, of the situation in which the revolution has placed us. A review of the several codes will show that every necessary and useful part of the least voluminous of them might be compressed into one tenth of the compass, and at the same time be rendered tenfold as perspicuous.

10. Mutability of the laws of the States.

This evil is intimately connected with the former yet deserves a distinct notice as it emphatically denotes a vicious legislation. We daily see laws repealed or superseded, before any trial can have been made of their merits: and even before a knowledge of them can have reached the remoter districts within which they were to operate. In the regulations of trade this instability becomes a snare not only to our citizens but to foreigners also.

11. Injustice of the laws of States.

If the multiplicity and mutability of laws prove a want of wisdom, their injustice betrays a defect still more alarming: more alarming not merely because it is a greater evil in itself, but because it brings more into question the fundamental principle of republican government, that the majority who rule in such governments, are the safest guardians both of public good and of private rights. To what causes is this evil to be ascribed?

These causes lie:

1. In the representative bodies.
2. In the people themselves.

　1. Representative appointments are sought from three motives.

　　1. ambition
　　2. personal interest.
　　3. public good.

Unhappily the two first are proved by experience to be most prevalent. Hence the candidates who feel them, particularly, the second, are most industrious, and most successful in pursuing their object: and forming often a majority in the legislative councils, with interested views, contrary to the interest, and views, of their constituents, join in a perfidious sacrifice of the latter to the former. A succeeding election it might be supposed, would displace the offenders, and repair the mischief. But how easily are base and selfish measures, masked by pretexts of public good and apparent expediency? How frequently will a repetition of the same arts and industry which succeeded in the first instance, again prevail on the unwary to misplace their confidence?

How frequently too will the honest but unenlightened representative be the dupe of a favorite leader, veiling his selfish views under the professions of public good, and varnishing his sophistical arguments with the glowing colors of popular eloquence?

　2. A still more fatal if not more frequent cause lies among the people themselves. All civilized societies are divided into different interests and factions, as they happen to be creditors or debtors—Rich or poor—husbandmen, merchants or manufacturers—members of different religious sects—followers of different political

leaders—inhabitants of different districts—owners of different kinds of property etc., etc. In republican government the majority, however composed, ultimately give the law. Whenever therefore an apparent interest or common passion unites a majority what is to restrain them from unjust violations of the rights and interests of the minority, or of individuals? Three motives only:

1. A prudent regard to their own good as involved in the general and permanent good of the community. This consideration although of decisive weight in itself, is found by experience to be too often unheeded. It is too often forgotten, by nations as well as by individuals that honesty is the best policy.

2. Respect for character. However strong this motive may be in individuals, it is considered as very insufficient to restrain them from injustice. In a multitude its efficacy is diminished in proportion to the number which is to share the praise or the blame. Besides, as it has reference to public opinion, which within a particular society, is the opinion of the majority, the standard is fixed by those whose conduct is to be measured by it. The public opinion without the society will be little respected by the people at large of any country. Individuals of extended views, and of national pride, may bring the public proceedings to this standard, but the example will never be followed by the multitude. Is it to be imagined that an ordinary citizen or even an assemblyman of Rhode Island in estimating the policy of paper money, ever considered or cared in what light the measure would be viewed in France or Holland; or even in Massachusetts or Connecticut? It was a sufficient temptation to both that it was for their interest: it was a sufficient sanction to the latter that it was popular in the state; to the former that it was so in the neighborhood.

3. Will religion, the only remaining motive, be a sufficient restraint? It is not pretended to be such on men individually considered. Will its effect be greater on them considered in an aggregate view? Quite the reverse. The conduct of every popular assembly acting on oath, the strongest of religious ties, proves that individuals join without remorse in acts,

against which their consciences would revolt if proposed to them under the like sanction, separately in their closets. When indeed religion is kindled into enthusiasm, its force like that of other passions, is increased by the sympathy of a multitude. But enthusiasm is only a temporary state of religion, and while it lasts will hardly be seen with pleasure at the helm of government. Besides as religion in its coolest state is not infallible, it may become a motive to oppression as well as a restraint from injustice. Place three individuals in a situation wherein the interest of each depends on the voice of the others, and give to two of them an interest opposed to the rights of the third? Will the latter be secure? The prudence of every man would shun the danger. The rules and forms of justice suppose and guard against it. Will two thousand in a like situation be less likely to encroach on the rights of one thousand? The contrary is witnessed by the notorious factions and oppressions which take place in corporate towns limited as the opportunities are, and in little republics when uncontrolled by apprehensions of external danger. If an enlargement of the sphere is found to lessen the insecurity of private rights, it is not because the impulse of a common interest or passion is less predominant in this case with the majority; but because a common interest or passion is less apt to be felt and the requisite combinations less easy to be formed by a great than by a small number. The society becomes broken into a greater variety of interests, of pursuits, of passions, which check each other, whilst those who may feel a common sentiment have less opportunity of communication and concert. It may be inferred that the inconveniences of popular states contrary to the prevailing theory are in proportion not to the extent, but to the narrowness of their limits.

The great desideratum in government is such a modification of the sovereignty as will render it sufficiently neutral between the different interests and factions, to control one part of the society from invading the rights of another, and at the same time sufficiently controlled itself, from setting up an interest adverse to that of the whole society. In absolute monarchies, the prince is sufficiently neutral towards his subjects, but frequently sacrifices their happiness to his ambition or his avarice. In small republics, the sovereign will is sufficiently controlled from such a sacrifice of the entire society, but is not sufficiently neutral towards the parts composing it. As a limited monarchy tempers the evils of an absolute one, so an extensive republic meliorates the administration of a small republic.

An auxiliary desideratum for the melioration of the republican form is such a process of elections as will most certainly extract from the mass of the society the purest and noblest characters which it contains; such as will at once feel most strongly the proper motives to pursue the end of their appointment, and be most capable to devise the proper means of attaining it.

12. Impotence of the laws of the States.

RULES TO BE OBSERVED AS THE STANDING ORDERS OF THE CONVENTION

("... whilst [the president] shall be speaking, none shall pass
between them, or hold discourse with another, or read a
book, pamphlet, or paper, printed or manuscript ...")

FEDERAL CONVENTION, PHILADELPHIA
MAY 28–29, 1787

> *For the most part, the fifty-five delegates to the Convention (who
> were from every state except Rhode Island, which declined to send
> anyone) were well-educated, experienced politicians. Even so, they
> needed and appreciated rules of conduct:* "Mr. Wythe reported
> from the committee (to whom the drawing up rules proper, in
> their opinion, to be observed by the Convention in their pro-
> ceedings, as standing orders, was referred), that the committee
> had drawn up the rules accordingly, and had directed him to
> report them to the house. And he read the report in his place,
> and afterwards delivered it in at the secretary's table, where the
> said rules were once read throughout, and then a second time,
> one by one; and upon the question, severally put thereupon,
> two of them were disagreed to; and the rest, with amendments
> to some of them, were agreed to by the house ..."[2]

Monday, May 28
"A house, to do business, shall consist of the deputies of not less than
seven states; and all questions shall be decided by the greater number
of these states which shall be fully represented. But a less number than
seven may adjourn from day to day.

---

[2] Jonathan Elliot. *The Debates in the Several State Conventions, on the Adoption of the Federal Constitution, as Recommended by the General Convention at Philadelphia, in 1787.* Vol. 1.
Philadelphia: J. B. Lippincott Co. 1888. 141–143.

"Immediately after the president shall have taken the chair, and the members their seats, the minutes of the preceding day shall be read by the secretary.

"Every member, rising to speak, shall address the president[3]; and, whilst he shall be speaking, none shall pass between them, or hold discourse with another, or read a book, pamphlet, or paper, printed or manuscript.

"And of two members rising at the same time, the president shall name him who shall be first heard.

"A member shall not speak oftener than twice, without special leave, upon the same question; and not the second time, before every other, who had been silent, shall have been heard, if he choose to speak upon the subject.

"A motion made and seconded shall be repeated, and if written, as it shall be when any member shall so require, read aloud, by the secretary, before it shall be debated; and may be withdrawn at any time before the vote upon it shall have been declared.

"Orders of the day shall be read next after the minutes, and either discussed or postponed before any other business shall be introduced.

"When a debate shall arise upon a question, no motion, other than to amend the question, to commit it, or to postpone the debate, shall be received.

"A question which is complicated shall, at the request of any member, be divided, and put separately upon the propositions of which it is compounded.

"The determination of a question, although fully debated, shall be postponed, if the deputies of any state desire it, until the next day.

"A writing which contains any matter brought on to be considered, shall be read once throughout, for information: then by paragraphs, to be debated; and again, with the amendments, if any, made on the second reading; and afterwards, the question shall be put upon the whole, amended, or approved in its original form, as the case shall be.

"That committees shall be appointed by ballot; and that the members who have the greatest number of ballots although not a majority of the votes present, be the committee. When two or more members have an equal number of votes, the member standing first on the list, in the order of taking down ballots, shall be preferred.

"A member may be called to order by any other member, as well as by the president, and may be allowed to explain his conduct, or expres-

---

[3] The President of the Convention was George Washington. While he was nominally addressed by each speaker, he rarely answered in turn.

sions, supposed to be reprehensible; and all questions of order shall be decided by the president, without appeal or debate.

"Upon a question to adjourn for the day, which may be made at any time, if it be seconded, the question shall be put without a debate.

"When the house shall adjourn, every member shall stand in his place until the president pass him.

"*Resolved*, That the said rules be observed as standing orders of the house."

A letter from sundry persons of the state of Rhode Island, addressed to the honorable the chairman of the General Convention, was presented to the chair by Mr. G. Morris; and, being read,—

"*Ordered*, That the said letter do lie upon the table for further consideration."

A motion was made by Mr. Butler, one of the deputies of South Carolina, that the house provide against interruption of business by absence of members, and against licentious publication of their proceedings.

Also, a motion was made by Mr. Spaight, one of the deputies of North Carolina, to provide that, on the one hand, the house may not be precluded, by a vote upon any question, from revising the subject matter of it, when they see cause; nor, on the other hand, be led too hastily to rescind a decision, which was the result of mature discussion.

"*Ordered*, That the said motions be referred to the consideration of the committee appointed, on Friday last, to draw up rules to be observed as the standing orders of the Convention; and that they do examine the matters thereof, and report thereupon to the house."

Adjourned till tomorrow at 10 o'clock, A. M.

Tuesday, May 29.

Mr. Wythe reported, from the committee to whom the motions made by Mr. Butler and Mr. Spaight were referred, that the committee had examined matters of the said motions, and had come to the following resolutions thereupon:—

"*Resolved*, That it is the opinion of this committee that provision be made for the purposes mentioned in the said motions; and to that end, the committee beg leave to propose, that the rules written under their resolution be added to the standing orders of the house."

And the said rules were once read throughout, and then, a second time, one by one; and on the question, severally put thereupon, were, with amendments to some of them, agreed to by the house; which rules, so agreed to, are as follow:—

"RULES.

"That no member be absent from the house, so as to interrupt the representation of the state, without leave.

"That committees do not sit whilst the house shall be, or ought to be, sitting.

"That no copy be taken of any entry on the Journal during the sitting of the house, without the leave of the house.

"That members only be permitted to inspect the Journal.

"That nothing spoken in the house be printed, or otherwise published, or communicated, without leave.

"That a motion to reconsider a matter which had been determined by a majority, may be made, with leave unanimously given, on the same day on which the vote passed; but otherwise not without one day's previous notice; in which last case, if the house agree to the reconsideration, some future day shall be assigned for that purpose.

"*Resolved*, That the said rules be added to the standing orders of the house."

THE "VIRGINIA PLAN," RESOLUTIONS OFFERED BY EDMUND RANDOLPH TO THE FEDERAL CONVENTION

("The Articles of the Confederation ought to be so corrected and enlarged as to accomplish the objects proposed by their institution . . .")

FEDERAL CONVENTION, PHILADELPHIA
MAY 29, 1787

James Madison prepared this plan, essentially a first-draft of the Constitution, but Edmund Randolph, the governor of Virginia, presented it. In its course over the next few months, the Virginia Plan would be challenged, revised, and modified in many details, but its primary direction remained.

1. *Resolved,* That the Articles of the Confederation ought to be so corrected and enlarged as to accomplish the objects proposed by their institution; namely, common defence, security of liberty, and general welfare.

2. *Resolved,* therefore, That the right of suffrage, in the national legislature, ought to be proportioned to the quotas of contribution, or to the number of free inhabitants, as the one or the other may seem best, in different cases.

3. *Resolved,* That the national legislature ought to consist of two branches.

4. *Resolved,* That the members of the first branch of national legislature ought to be elected by the people of the several states, every _____, for the term of _____, to be of the age of years, at least; to receive liberal stipends, by which they may be compensated for the devotion of their time to the public service; to be ineligible to any office established by a particular state, or under the authority of the United States (except those peculiarly belonging to the functions of the first branch) during the term of service and for the space of after its expira-

tion; to be incapable of reelection for the space of after the expiration of their term of service; and to be subject to recall.

5. *Resolved*, That the members of the second branch of the national legislature ought to be elected by those of the first, out of a proper number of persons nominated by the individual legislatures, to be of the age of years, at least; to hold their offices for a term sufficient to insure their independency; to receive liberal stipends, by which they may be compensated for the devotion of their time to the public service; and to be ineligible to any office established by a particular state, or under the authority of the United States (except those particularly belonging to the functions of the second branch) during the term of service; and for the space of after the expiration thereof.

6. *Resolved*, That each branch ought to possess the right of originating acts; that the national legislature ought to be empowered to enjoy the legislative right vested in Congress by the Confederation; and, moreover, to legislate in all cases to which the separate states are incompetent, or in which the harmony of the United States may be interrupted by the exercise of individual legislation; to negative all laws passed by the several states, contravening, in the opinion of the national legislature, the articles of union, or any treaty subsisting under the authority of the Union; and to call forth the force of the Union against any member of the Union failing to fulfill its duty under the articles thereof.

7. *Resolved*, That a national executive be instituted, to be chosen by the national legislature for the term of years, to receive punctually, at stated times, a fixed compensation for the services rendered, in which no increase or diminution shall be made, so as to affect the magistracy existing at the time of the increase or diminution; to be ineligible a second time; and that, besides a general authority to execute the national laws, it ought to enjoy the executive rights vested in Congress by the Confederation.

8. *Resolved*, That the executive, and a convenient number of the national judiciary, ought to compose a council of revision, with authority to examine every act of the national legislature, before it shall operate, and every act of a particular legislature, before a negative thereon shall be final; and that the dissent of the said council shall amount to a rejection, unless the act of the national legislature be again passed, or that of a particular legislature be again negatived by of the members of each branch.

9. *Resolved*, That a national judiciary be established to hold their offices during good behavior, and to receive punctually, at stated times, a fixed compensation for their services, in which no increase or dimi-

nution shall be made, so as to affect the persons actually in office at the time of such increase or diminution. That the jurisdiction of the inferior tribunals shall be to hear and determine in the first instance, and of the supreme tribunal to hear and determine in the *dernier resort*, all piracies and felonies on the seas; captures from an enemy; cases in which foreigners, or citizens of other states, applying to such jurisdictions, may be interested, or which respect the collection of the national revenue; impeachments of any national officer; and questions which involve the national peace or harmony.

10. *Resolved*, That provision ought to be made for the admission of states, lawfully arising within the limits of the United States, whether from a voluntary junction of government or territory, or otherwise, with the consent of a number of voices in the national legislature less than the whole.

11. *Resolved*, That a republican government and the territory of each state (except in the instance of a voluntary junction of government and territory) ought to be guarantied by the United States to each state.

12. *Resolved*, That provision ought to be made for the continuance of Congress, and their authorities and privileges, until a given day, after the reform of the articles of union shall be adopted, and for the completion of all their engagements.

13. *Resolved*, That provision ought to be made for the amendment of the articles of union, whensoever it shall seem necessary; and that the assent of the national legislature ought not to be required thereto.

14. *Resolved*, That the legislative, executive, and judiciary powers within the several states ought to be bound by oath to support the articles of union.

15. *Resolved*, That the amendments, which shall be offered to the Confederation by the Convention, ought, at a proper time or times, after the approbation of Congress, to be submitted to an assembly or assemblies of representatives, recommended by the several legislatures, to be expressly chosen by the people to consider and decide thereon.

DEBATE IN THE CONSTITUTIONAL CONVENTION ON SUFFRAGE: ELBRIDGE GERRY, GEORGE MASON, JAMES WILSON, JAMES MADISON, EDMUND RANDOLPH, AND OTHERS

("Mr. Wilson contended strenuously for drawing the most numerous branch of the legislature immediately from the people")

FEDERAL CONVENTION, PHILADELPHIA
MAY 31, 1787

The convention delegates did not take for granted the people's right to vote for members of the House of Representatives (in fact, the people did not vote for their U.S. senators until the 17th Amendment passed in 1913), and suffrage was a matter of pointed debate.

James Madison's Notes on the Debates in the Federal Convention of 1787 *are the most complete record of what happened and what was said during this spring and summer in Philadelphia; his notes were not published until 1840, after he and all of his colleagues had died. The debates as recorded here and in the next several documents are a mixture of Madison's paraphrase, summary, and direct quotation.*

In committee of the whole on Mr. Randolph's propositions.

The third resolution, "that the national legislature ought to consist of two branches," was agreed to without debate or dissent, except that of Pennsylvania, given probably from complaisance to Dr. Franklin, who was understood to be partial to a single house of legislation.

Resolution 4, first clause, "that the members of the first branch of the national legislature ought to be elected by the people of the several states," being taken up, MR. SHERMAN opposed the election by the people, insisting that it ought to be by the state legislatures. The people, he said, immediately should have as little to do as may be about the government. They want information and are constantly liable to be misled.

MR. GERRY: The evils we experience flow from the excess of democracy. The people do not want virtue, but are the dupes of pretended patriots. In Massachusetts it had been fully confirmed by experience that they are daily misled into the most baneful measures and opinions by the false reports circulated by designing men, and which no one on the spot can refute. One principal evil arises from the want of due provision for those employed in the administration of government. It would seem to be a maxim of democracy to starve the public servants. He mentioned the popular clamor in Massachusetts for the reduction of salaries and the attack made on that of the governor, though secured by the spirit of the Constitution itself. He had, he said, been too republican heretofore: he was still however republican, but had been taught by experience the danger of the leveling spirit.

MR. MASON argued strongly for an election of the larger branch by the people. It was to be the grand depository of the democratic principle of the government. It was, so to speak, to be our House of Commons. It ought to know and sympathize with every part of the community; and ought therefore to be taken not only from different parts of the whole republic, but also from different districts of the larger members of it, which had in several instances, particularly in Virginia, different interests and views arising from difference of produce, of habits, etc. He admitted that we had been too democratic but was afraid we should incautiously run into the opposite extreme. We ought to attend to the rights of every class of the people. He had often wondered at the indifference of the superior classes of society to this dictate of humanity and policy; considering that however affluent their circumstances, or elevated their situations, might be, the course of a few years, not only might but certainly would, distribute their posterity throughout the lowest classes of society. Every selfish motive therefore, every family attachment, ought to recommend such a system of policy as would provide no less carefully for the rights and happiness of the lowest than of the highest orders of citizens.

MR. WILSON contended strenuously for drawing the most numerous branch of the legislature immediately from the people. He was for raising the federal pyramid to a considerable altitude, and for that reason wished to give it as broad a basis as possible. No government could long subsist without the confidence of the people. In a republican government this confidence was peculiarly essential. He also thought it wrong to increase the weight of the state legislatures by making them the electors of the national legislature. All interference between the general and local governments should be obviated as much as possible. On examination it would be found that the opposition of states to federal measures had proceeded much more from the officers of the states, than from the people at large.

Mr. Madison considered the popular election of one branch of the national legislature as essential to every plan of free government. He observed that in some of the states one branch of the legislature was composed of men already removed from the people by an intervening body of electors. That if the first branch of the general legislature should be elected by the state legislatures, the second branch elected by the first, the executive by the second together with the first, and other appointments again made for subordinate purposes by the executive, the people would be lost sight of altogether; and the necessary sympathy between them and their rulers and officers too little felt. He was an advocate for the policy of refining the popular appointments by successive filtrations, but thought it might be pushed too far. He wished the expedient to be resorted to only in the appointment of the second branch of the legislature, and in the executive and judiciary branches of the government. He thought, too, that the great fabric to be raised would be more stable and durable, if it should rest on the solid foundation of the people themselves, than if it should stand merely on the pillars of the legislatures.

Mr. Gerry did not like the election by the people. The maxims taken from the British constitution were often fallacious when applied to our situation, which was extremely different. Experience, he said, had shown that the state legislatures drawn immediately from the people did not always possess their confidence. He had no objection however to an election by the people if it were so qualified that men of honor and character might not be unwilling to be joined in the appointments. He seemed to think the people might nominate a certain number out of which the state legislatures should be bound to choose.

Mr. Butler thought an election by the people an impracticable mode.

On the question for an election of the first branch of the national legislature by the people: Massachusetts: ay; Connecticut: divided; New York: ay; New Jersey: no; Pennsylvania: ay; Delaware: divided; Virginia: ay; North Carolina: ay; South Carolina: no; Georgia: ay.

The remaining clauses of the fourth resolution relating to the qualifications of members of the national legislature, being postponed, unanimously, as entering too much into detail for general propositions, the committee proceeded to resolution five, "that the second (or senatorial) branch of the national legislature ought to be chosen by the first branch out of persons nominated by the state legislatures."

MR. SPAIGHT contended that the second branch ought to be chosen by the state legislatures and moved an amendment to that effect. MR. BUTLER apprehended that the taking so many powers out of the hands of the states, as was proposed, tended to destroy all that balance and security of interests among the states which it was necessary to preserve; and called on Mr. Randolph, the mover of the propositions, to explain the extent of his ideas, and particularly the number of members he meant to assign to this second branch.

MR. RANDOLPH observed that he had at the time of offering his propositions stated his ideas as far as the nature of general propositions required; that details made no part of the plan, and could not perhaps with propriety have been introduced. If he was to give an opinion as to the number of the second branch, he should say that it ought to be much smaller than that of the first; so small as to be exempt from the passionate proceedings to which numerous assemblies are liable. He observed that the general object was to provide a cure for the evils under which the U. S. labored; that in tracing these evils to their origin every man had found it in the turbulence and follies of democracy; that some check therefore was to be sought for against this tendency of our governments; and that a good senate seemed most likely to answer the purpose.

MR. KING reminded the committee that the choice of the second branch as proposed (by Mr. Spaight) viz. by the state legislatures would be impracticable, unless it was to be very numerous, or the idea of proportion among the states was to be disregarded. According to this idea, there must be eighty or a hundred members to entitle Delaware to the choice of one of them.

MR. SPAIGHT withdrew his motion.

MR. WILSON opposed both a nomination by the state legislatures and an election by the first branch of the national legislature, because the second branch of the latter ought to be independent of both. He thought both branches of the national legislature ought to be chosen by the people, but was not prepared with a specific proposition. He suggested the mode of choosing the Senate of New York — to wit, of uniting several election districts, for one branch, in choosing members for the other branch — as a good model.

MR. MADISON observed that such a mode would destroy the influence of the smaller states associated with larger ones in the same district; as the latter would choose from within themselves, although better men might be found in the former. The election of senators in Virginia, where large and small counties were often formed into one district for the purpose, had illustrated this consequence. Local partiality would often prefer a resident within the county or state to a candidate of superior merit residing out of it. Less merit also in a resident would be more known throughout his own state.

MR. SHERMAN favored an election of one member by each of the state legislatures.

MR. PINCKNEY moved to strike out the "nomination by the state legislatures."

On this question: Massachusetts, Connecticut, New York, New Jersey, Pennsylvania, Virginia, North Carolina, South Carolina, Georgia, *no*—nine; Delaware *divided*.

On the whole question for electing by the first branch out of nominations by the state legislatures: Massachusetts, Virginia, South Carolina, *aye*—three; Connecticut, New York, New Jersey, Pennsylvania, Delaware, North Carolina, Georgia, *no*—seven.

So the clause was disagreed to and a chasm left in this part of the plan.

DEBATE IN THE CONSTITUTIONAL CONVENTION ON EXECUTIVE POWER: CHARLES PINCKNEY, JAMES WILSON, JAMES MADISON, AND OTHERS

("Mr. Madison thought it would be proper, before a choice
should be made between a unity and a plurality in the
executive, to fix the extent of the executive authority")

FEDERAL CONVENTION, PHILADELPHIA
JUNE 1 AND JUNE 4, 1787

> *This debate ranges over many points about the Executive Branch, among them the number of executives, his length of service, and the executive's power to veto and to conduct war. (The Constitution would settle one of these topics thusly:* "He shall have Power, by and with the Advice and Consent of the Senate, to make Treaties, provided two thirds of the Senators present concur; and he shall nominate, and by and with the Advice and Consent of the Senate, shall appoint Ambassadors, other public Ministers and Consuls, Judges of the supreme Court, and all other Officers of the United States . . ." *Article II, Section 1.)*

June 1

The Committee of the whole proceeded to Resolution 7 "that a national Executive be instituted, to be chosen by the national Legislature-for the term of ___ years, etc., to be ineligible thereafter, to possess the executive powers of Congress, etc."

MR. PINCKNEY was for a vigorous executive but was afraid the executive powers of the existing Congress might extend to peace and war, etc., which would render the executive a monarchy of the worst kind, to wit, an elective one.

MR. WILSON moved that the executive consist of a single person.

MR. PINCKNEY seconded the motion, so as to read "that a national executive to consist of a single person, be instituted."

A considerable pause ensuing and the chairman asking if he should put the question, DR. FRANKLIN observed that it was a point of great importance and wished that the gentlemen would deliver their sentiments on it before the question was put.

MR. RUTLEDGE animadverted on the shyness of gentlemen on this and other subjects. He said it looked as if they supposed themselves precluded by having frankly disclosed their opinions from afterwards changing them, which he did not take to be at all the case. He said he was for vesting the executive power in a single person, though he was not for giving him the power of war and peace. A single man would feel the greatest responsibility and administer the public affairs best.

MR. SHERMAN said he considered the executive magistracy as nothing more than an institution for carrying the will of the legislature into effect, that the person or persons ought to be appointed by and accountable to the legislature only, which was the depositary of the supreme will of the society. As they were the best judges of the business which ought to be done by the executive department, and consequently of the number necessary from time to time for doing it, he wished the number might not be fixed but that the legislature should be at liberty to appoint one or more as experience might dictate.

MR. WILSON preferred a single magistrate, as giving most energy dispatch and responsibility to the office. He did not consider the prerogatives of the British monarchs as a proper guide in defining the executive powers. Some of these prerogatives were of legislative nature, among others, that of war and peace. The only powers he conceived strictly executive were those of executing the laws, and appointing officers, not appertaining to and appointed by the legislature.

MR. GERRY favored the policy of annexing a council to the executive in order to give weight and inspire confidence.

MR. RANDOLPH strenuously opposed a unity in the executive magistracy. He regarded it as the fetus of monarchy. We had, he said, no motive to be governed by the British government as our prototype. He did not mean however to throw censure on that excellent fabric. If we were in a situation to copy it he did not know that he should be opposed to it; but the fixed genius of the people of America required a different form of government. He could not see why the great requisites for the executive department—vigor, dispatch and responsibility—could not be found in three men, as well as in one man. The executive ought to be independent. It ought therefore in order to support its independence to consist of more than one.

MR. WILSON said that unity in the executive instead of being the fetus of monarchy would be the best safeguard against tyranny. He repeated that he was not governed by the British model which was inapplicable to the situation of this country; the extent of which was so great, and the manners so republican, that nothing but a great confederated republic would do for it. Mr. Wilson's motion for a single magistrate was postponed by common consent, the committee seeming unprepared for any decision on it; and the first part of the clause agreed to, namely, "that a national executive be instituted."

MR. MADISON thought it would be proper, before a choice should be made between a unity and a plurality in the executive, to fix the extent of the executive authority; that as certain powers were in their nature executive, and must be given to that department, whether administered by one or more persons, a definition of their extent would assist the judgment in determining how far they might be safely entrusted to a single officer. He accordingly moved that so much of the clause before the committee as related to the powers of the executive should be struck out and that after the words "that a national executive ought to be instituted," there be inserted the words following, namely, "with power to carry into effect the national laws, to appoint to offices in cases not otherwise provided for, and to execute such other powers 'not legislative nor judiciary in their nature,' as may from time to time be delegated by the national legislature." The words "not legislative nor judiciary in their nature" were added to the proposed amendment in consequence of a suggestion by General Pinckney that improper powers might otherwise be delegated.

MR. WILSON seconded this motion.

MR. PINCKNEY moved to amend the amendment by striking out the last member of it; namely: "and to execute such other powers not legislative nor judiciary in their nature as may from time to time be delegated." He said they were unnecessary, the object of them being included in the "power to carry into effect the national laws."

MR. RANDOLPH seconded the motion.

MR. MADISON did not know that the words were absolutely necessary, or even the preceding words, "to appoint to offices, etc.," the whole being perhaps included in the first member of the proposition. He did not however see any inconveniency in retaining them, and cases might happen in which they might serve to prevent doubts and misconstructions.

In consequence of the motion of MR. PINCKNEY, the question on MR. MADISON's motion was divided; and the words objected to by MR. PINCKNEY struck out; by the votes of Connecticut, New York, New Jersey, Pennsylvania, Delaware, North Carolina, and Georgia — *against*. Massachusetts, Virginia, South Carolina the preceding part of the motion being first *agreed* to; Connecticut *divided*, all the other states in the *affirmative*. The next clause in Resolution 7, relating to the mode of appointing and the duration of the executive being under consideration,

MR. WILSON said he was almost unwilling to declare the mode which he wished to take place, being apprehensive that it might appear chimerical. He would say however at least that in theory he was for an election by the people. Experience, particularly in New York and Massachusetts, showed that an election of the first magistrate by the people at large was both a convenient and successful mode. The objects of choice in such cases must be persons whose merits have general notoriety.

MR. SHERMAN was for the appointment by the legislature, and for making him absolutely dependent on that body, as it was the will of that which was to be executed. An independence of the executive on the supreme legislature was, in his opinion, the very essence of tyranny if there was any such thing.

MR. WILSON moves that the blank for the term of duration should be filled with three years, observing at the same time that he preferred this short period, on the supposition that a reeligibility would be provided for.

MR. PINCKNEY moves for seven years.

MR. SHERMAN was for three years, and against the doctrine of rotation as throwing out of office the men best qualified to execute its duties.

MR. MASON was for seven years at least, and for prohibiting a reeligibility as the best expedient both for preventing the effect of a false complaisance on the side of the legislature towards unfit characters; and a temptation on the side of the executive to intrigue with the legislature for a reappointment.

MR. BEDFORD was strongly opposed to so long a term as seven years. He begged the committee to consider what the situation of the country would be, in case the first magistrate should be saddled on it for such a period and it should be found on trial that he did not possess the qualifications ascribed to him, or should lose them after his appointment. An impeachment he said would be no cure for this evil, as an impeachment would reach misfeasance only, not incapacity. He was for a triennial election, and for an ineligibility after a period of nine years.

On the question for seven years, New York, New Jersey, Pennsylvania, Delaware, Virginia, *aye*—five; Connecticut, North Carolina, South Carolina, Georgia, *no*—four; Massachusetts, *divided*. There being five ays, four noes, one divided, a question was asked whether a majority had voted in the affirmative? The President decided that it was an affirmative vote.

The mode of appointing the executive was the next question.

Mr. Wilson renewed his declarations in favor of an appointment by the people. He wished to derive not only both branches of the legislature from the people, without the intervention of the state legislatures but the executive also; in order to make them as independent as possible of each other, as well as of the states.

Mr. Mason favors the idea, but thinks it impracticable. He wishes however that Mr. Wilson might have time to digest it into his own form, the clause "to be chosen by the national legislature" was accordingly postponed.

Mr. Rutledge suggests an election of the executive by the second branch only of the national legislature.

The committee then rose and the house adjourned.

June 4

In committee of the whole, the question was resumed on motion of Mr. Pinckney seconded by Mr. Wilson, "shall the *blank* for the number of the executive be filled with a single person?"

Mr. Wilson was in favor of the motion. It had been opposed by the gentleman from Virginia (*Mr. Randolph*), but the arguments used had not convinced him. He observed that the objections of Mr. Randolph were leveled not so much against the measure itself, as against its unpopularity. If he could suppose that it would occasion a rejection of the plan of which it should form a part, though the part was an important one, yet he would give it up rather than lose the whole. On examination he could see no evidence of the alleged antipathy of the people. On the contrary he was persuaded that it does not exist. All know that a single magistrate is not a king. One fact has great weight with him. All the thirteen states, though agreeing in scarce any other instance, agree in placing a single magistrate at the head of the government. The idea of three heads has taken place in none. The degree of power is indeed different; but there are no coordinate heads. In addition to his former reasons for preferring a unity, he would mention another. The tranquility not less than the vigor of the government, he thought, would be favored by it. Among three equal members, he foresaw nothing but uncontrolled, continued, and violent animosities, which would not only interrupt the public administration, but diffuse their poison through the other branches of government, through the states, and at length through the people at large. If the members were to be unequal in power the principle of the opposition to the unity was given up. If equal, the making them an odd number would not be a remedy. In courts of justice there are two sides only to a question. In the legislative and executive departments questions have commonly many sides. Each member therefore might espouse a separate one and no two agree.

MR. SHERMAN. This matter is of great importance and ought to be well considered before it is determined. Mr. Wilson, he said, had observed that in each state a single magistrate was placed at the head of the government. It was so he admitted, and properly so, and he wished the same policy to prevail in the federal government. But then it should be also remarked that in all the states there was a council of advice, without which the first magistrate could not act. A council he thought necessary to make the establishment acceptable to the people. Even in Great Britain the king has a council; and though he appoints it himself, its advice has its weight with him, and attracts the confidence of the people.

MR. WILLIAMSON asks Mr. Wilson whether he means to annex a council.

MR. WILSON means to have no council, which oftener serves to cover than prevent malpractices.

MR. GERRY was at a loss to discover the policy of three members for the executive. It would be extremely inconvenient in many instances, particularly in military matters, whether relating to the militia, an army, or a navy. It would be a general with three heads.

On the question for a single executive it was agreed to: Massachusetts, Connecticut, Pennsylvania, Virginia (Mr. Randolph and Mr. Blair, *no*; Doctor McClurg, Mr. Madison, and General Washington, *aye*; Colonel Mason being *no*, but not in the House, Mr. Wythe, *aye*, but gone home), North Carolina, South Carolina, Georgia, *aye*—seven; New York, Delaware, Maryland, *no*—three.

[. . .]

MR. GERRY's proposition being now before committee, MR. WILSON and MR. HAMILTON move that the last part of it (namely, "which shall not be afterwards passed unless by _____ parts of each branch of the national legislature") be struck out, so as to give the executive an absolute negative on the laws. There was no danger, they thought, of such a power being too much exercised. It was mentioned by MR. HAMILTON that the King of Great Britain had not exerted his negative since the revolution.

MR. GERRY sees no necessity for so great a control over the legislature as the best men in the community would be comprised in the two branches of it.

DR. FRANKLIN said he was sorry to differ from his colleague for whom he had a very great respect, on any occasion, but he could not help it on this. He had had some experience of this check in the executive on the legislature, under the proprietary government of

Pennsylvania. The negative of the governor was constantly made use of to extort money. No good law whatever could be passed without a private bargain with him. An increase of his salary, or some donation, was always made a condition; till at last it became the regular practice, to have orders in his favor on the treasury, presented along with the bills to be signed, so that he might actually receive the former before he should sign the latter. When the Indians were scalping the western people, and notice of it arrived, the concurrence of the governor in the means of self-defense could not be got till it was agreed that his estate should be exempted from taxation: so that the people were to fight for the security of his property, whilst he was to bear no share of the burden. This was a mischievous sort of check. If the executive was to have a council, such a power would be less objectionable. It was true the King of Great Britain had not, as was said, exerted his negative since the revolution; but that matter was easily explained. The bribes and emoluments now given to the members of Parliament rendered it unnecessary, everything being done according to the will of the ministers. He was afraid, if a negative should be given as proposed, that more power and money would be demanded, till at last enough would be gotten to influence and bribe the legislature into a complete subjection to the will of the executive.

Mr. Sherman was against enabling any one man to stop the will of the whole. No one man could be found so far above all the rest in wisdom. He thought we ought to avail ourselves of his wisdom in revising the laws, but not permit him to overrule the decided and cool opinions of the legislature.

Mr. Madison supposed that if a proper proportion of each branch should be required to overrule the objections of the executive, it would answer the same purpose as an absolute negative. It would rarely if ever happen that the executive, constituted as ours is proposed to be, would have firmness enough to resist the legislature, unless backed by a certain part of the body itself. The King of Great Britain with all his splendid attributes would not be able to withstand the unanimous and eager wishes of both houses of Parliament. To give such a prerogative would certainly be obnoxious to the temper of this country — its present temper at least.

Mr. Wilson believed as others did that this power would seldom be used. The legislature would know that such a power existed, and would refrain from such laws, as it would be sure to defeat. Its silent operation would therefore preserve harmony and prevent mischief. The case of Pennsylvania formerly was very different from its present case. The executive was not then as now to be appointed by the people. It will not in this case as in the one cited be supported by the head of a great empire, actuated by a different and sometimes opposite interest. The salary too is now proposed to be fixed by the Constitution, or if Dr. Franklin's idea should be adopted all salary whatever interdicted. The requiring a large proportion of each House to over-rule the executive check might do in peaceable times; but there might be tempestuous moments in which animosities may run high between the executive and legislative branches, and in which the former ought to be able to defend itself.

Mr. Butler had been in favor of a single executive magistrate; but could he have entertained an idea that a complete negative on the laws was to be given him he certainly should have acted very differently. It had been observed that in all countries the executive power is in a constant course of increase. This was certainly the case in Great Britain. Gentlemen seemed to think that we had nothing to apprehend from an abuse of the executive power. But why might not a Cataline or a Cromwell arise in this country as well as in others?

Mr. Bedford was opposed to every check on the legislative, even the council of revision first proposed. He thought it would be sufficient to mark out in the Constitution the boundaries to the legislative authority, which would give all the requisite security to the rights of the other departments. The representatives of the people were the best judges of what was for their interest, and ought to be under no external control whatever. The two branches would produce a sufficient control within the legislature itself.

Mr. Mason observed that a vote had already passed, he found (he was out at the time), for vesting the executive powers in a single person. Among these powers was that of appointing to offices in certain cases. The probable abuses of a negative had been well explained by Dr. Franklin, as proved by experience the best of all tests. Will not the same door be opened here? The executive may refuse its assent to necessary measures till new appointments shall be referred to him; and having by degrees engrossed all these into his own hands, the American executive, like the British, will by bribery and influence save himself the trouble and odium of exerting his negative afterwards. We are, Mr. Chairman, going very far in this business. We are not indeed constituting a British government, but a more dangerous monarchy, an elective one. We are introducing a new principle into our system, and not necessary as in the British government, where the executive has greater rights to defend. Do gentlemen mean to pave the way to hereditary monarchy? Do they flatter themselves that the people will ever consent to such an innovation? If they do, I venture to tell them, they are mistaken. The people never will consent. And do, gentlemen, consider the danger of delay, and the still greater danger of a rejection, not for a moment but forever, of the plan which shall be proposed to them. Notwithstanding the oppressions and injustice experienced among us from democracy, the genius of the people is in favor of it, and the genius of the people must be consulted.

He could not but consider the federal system as in effect dissolved by the appointment of this convention to devise a better one. And do, gentlemen, look forward to the dangerous interval between the extinction of an old, and the establishment of a new government and to the scenes of confusion which may ensue. He hoped that nothing like a monarchy would ever be attempted in this country. A hatred to its oppressions had carried the people through the late revolution. Will it not be enough to enable the executive to suspend offensive laws, till they shall be coolly revised, and the objections to them overruled by a greater majority than was required in the first instance? He never could agree to give up all the rights of the people to a single magistrate. If more than one had been fixed on, greater powers might have been entrusted to the executive. He hoped this attempt to give such powers would have its weight hereafter as an argument for increasing the number of the executive.

DR. FRANKLIN. A gentleman from South Carolina (*Mr. Butler*) a day or two ago called our attention to the case of the United Netherlands. He wished the gentleman had been a little fuller, and had gone back to the original of that government. The people being under great obligations to the Prince of Orange, whose wisdom and bravery had saved them, chose him for the stadtholder. He did very well. Inconveniences, however, were felt from his powers, which growing more and more oppressive, they were at length set aside. Still, however, there was a party for the Prince of Orange, which descended to his son, who excited insurrections, spilt a great deal of blood, murdered the DeWitts, and got the powers revested in the stadtholder. Afterwards another prince had power to excite insurrections and to make the stadtholdership hereditary. And the present stadtholder is ready to wade through a bloody civil war to the establishment of a monarchy. Colonel Mason had mentioned the circumstance of appointing officers. He knew how that point would be managed. No new appointment would be suffered as heretofore in Pennsylvania unless it be referred to the executive, so that all profitable offices will be at his disposal. The first man put at the helm will be a good one. Nobody knows what sort may come afterwards. The executive will be always increasing here, as elsewhere, till it ends in a monarchy.

On the question for striking out so as to give executive an absolute negative: Massachusetts, Connecticut, New York, Pennsylvania, Delaware, Maryland, Virginia, North Carolina, South Carolina, Georgia, *no*—ten.

DEBATE IN THE CONSTITUTIONAL CONVENTION ON SMALL STATES VERSUS THE LARGE STATES: SPEECH BY GUNNING BEDFORD, JR., OF DELAWARE

("... the larger states proceed as if our eyes were already perfectly blinded")

FEDERAL CONVENTION, PHILADELPHIA
JUNE 30, 1787

The "Great Compromise" (or Connecticut Compromise) that would come on July 16 involved apportioning equal representation in the Senate and proportional representation in the House of Representatives. Gunning Bedford, Jr., was a lawyer with a hot-tempered manner that riled some of his colleagues at the convention. In this impassioned speech, he gave voice, in any case, to the concerns of the smaller states and eventually helped Delaware become the first state to ratify the Constitution.

That all the states at present are equally sovereign and independent has been asserted from every quarter of this house. Our deliberations here are a confirmation of the position; and I may add to it, that each of them acts from interested and many from ambitious motives. Look at the votes which have been given on the floor of this house, and it will be found that their numbers, wealth, and local views have actuated their determinations, and that the larger states proceed as if our eyes were already perfectly blinded. Impartiality, with them, is already out of the question; the reported plan is their political creed, and they support it, right or wrong. Even the diminutive state of Georgia has an eye to her future wealth and greatness. South Carolina, puffed up with the possession of her wealth and negroes, and North Carolina are all, from different views, united with the great states. And these latter, although it is said they can never from interested views form a coalition, we find closely united in one scheme of interest and ambition (notwithstanding they endeavor to amuse us with the purity of their principle and

51

the rectitude of their intentions) in asserting that the general government must be drawn from an equal representation of the people.

Pretences to support ambition are never wanting. Their cry is, "Where is the danger?" And they insist that although the powers of the general government will be increased, yet it will be for the good of the whole; and although the three great states form nearly a majority of the people of America, they never will hurt or injure the lesser states. I do not, gentlemen, trust you. If you possess the power, the abuse of it could not be checked; and what then would prevent you from exercising it to our destruction? You gravely allege that there is no danger of combination, and triumphantly ask, "How could combinations be effected? The large states," you say, "all differ in productions and commerce; and experience shows that, instead of combinations, they would be rivals, and counteract the views of one another." This, I repeat, is language calculated only to amuse us. Yes, sir, the larger states will be rivals, but not against each other — they will be rivals against the rest of the states. But it is urged that such a government would suit the people, and that its principles are equitable and just. How often has this argument been refuted, when applied to a federal government! The small states never can agree to the Virginia plan; and why, then, is it still urged? But it is said that it is not expected that the state governments will approve the proposed system, and that this house must directly carry it to the people for their approbation! Is it come to this, then, that the sword must decide this controversy, and that the horrors of war must be added to the rest of our misfortunes? But what have the people already said? "We find the Confederation defective. Go, and give additional powers to the Confederation — give to it the imposts, regulation of trade, power to collect the taxes, and the means to discharge our foreign and domestic debts."

Can we not, then, as their delegates, agree upon these points? As their ambassadors, can we not clearly grant those powers? Why, then, when we are met, must entire distinct and new grounds be taken, and a government of which the people had no idea be instituted? And are we to be told, if we won't agree to it, it is the last moment of our deliberations? I say, it is indeed the last moment, if we do not agree to this assumption of power. The states will never again be entrapped into a measure like this. The people will say, The small states would confederate, and grant further powers to Congress; but you, the large states, would not. Then the fault would be yours, and all the nations of the earth will justify us. But what is to become of our public debts, if we dissolve the Union? Where is your plighted faith? Will you crush the smaller states, or must they be left unmolested? Sooner than be ruined, there are foreign powers who will take us by the hand.

I say not this to threaten or intimidate, but that we should reflect seriously before we act. If we once leave this floor, and solemnly renounce your new project, what will be the consequence? You will annihilate your federal government, and ruin must stare you in the face. Let us, then, do what is in our power—amend and enlarge the Confederation, but not alter the federal system. The people expect this, and no more. We all agree in the necessity of a more efficient government—and cannot this be done? Although my state is small, I know and respect its rights as much, at least, as those who have the honor to represent any of the larger states.

DEBATE IN THE CONSTITUTIONAL CONVENTION ON THE SLAVE TRADE: LUTHER MARTIN, JOHN RUTLEDGE, GEORGE MASON, CHARLES PINCKNEY, AND OTHERS

("... it was inconsistent with the principles of the revolution, and dishonorable to the American character, to have such a feature in the Constitution")

FEDERAL CONVENTION, PHILADELPHIA
AUGUST 21–22, 1787

> *Article I, Section 9, of the Constitution* ("The Migration or Importation of such Persons as any of the States now existing shall think proper to admit, shall not be prohibited by the Congress prior to the Year one thousand eight hundred and eight, but a Tax or duty may be imposed on such Importation, not exceeding ten dollars for each Person") *does not contain the words "slavery" or "slave," in part because slavery was even then a shameful practice, highlighting all by itself the hypocrisy of the enlightened Christian men of the Constitutional Convention, many of whom prided themselves on having fought for independence and individual liberty. Representatives from South Carolina, notably Charles Pinckney, threatened that attempts to outlaw or limit slavery would dissolve South Carolina's, North Carolina's, and Georgia's agreement to the new document. Several delegates advocated ducking this topic as a moral issue, preferring to proceed as if slavery were an entrenched, untouchable business and that the people enslaved could be considered when divvying political power (the infamous "three-fifths" rule) but not as individual souls.*

Tuesday, August 21
  On the question on Article 7, Section 4, as far as to "no tax shall be laid on exports," it passed in the affirmative,—

Massachusetts, Connecticut, Maryland, Virginia (General Washington and Mr. Madison, *no*), North Carolina, South Carolina, Georgia, *aye*—seven; New Hampshire, New Jersey, Pennsylvania, Delaware, *no*—four.

MR. L. MARTIN proposed to vary Article 7, Section 4, so as to allow a prohibition or tax on the importation of slaves. In the first place, as five slaves are to be counted as three freemen, in the apportionment of Representatives, such a clause would leave an encouragement to this traffic. In the second place, slaves weakened one part of the Union, which the other parts were bound to protect; the privilege of importing them was therefore unreasonable. And in the third place, it was inconsistent with the principles of the revolution, and dishonorable to the American character, to have such a feature in the Constitution.

MR. RUTLEDGE did not see how the importation of slaves could be encouraged by this section. He was not apprehensive of insurrections, and would readily exempt the other states from the obligation to protect the Southern against them. Religion and humanity had nothing to do with this question. Interest alone is the governing principle with nations. The true question at present is, whether the Southern states shall or shall not be parties to the Union. If the Northern states consult their interest, they will not oppose the increase of slaves, which will increase the commodities of which they will become the carriers.

MR. ELLSWORTH was for leaving the clause as it stands. Let every state import what it pleases. The morality or wisdom of slavery are considerations belonging to the states themselves. What enriches a part enriches the whole, and the states are the best judges of their particular interest. The old Confederation had not meddled with this point; and he did not see any greater necessity for bringing it within the policy of the new one.

MR. PINCKNEY. South Carolina can never receive the plan if it prohibits the slave-trade. In every proposed extension of the powers of Congress, that state has expressly and watchfully excepted that of meddling with the importation of negroes. If the states be all left at liberty on this subject, South Carolina may perhaps, by degrees, do of herself what is wished, as Virginia and Maryland already have done.

Adjourned.

Wednesday, August 22

In Convention.—Article 7, Section 4, was resumed.

MR. SHERMAN was for leaving the clause as it stands. He disapproved of the slave trade; yet as the states were now possessed of the right to import slaves, as the public good did not require it to be taken from them, and as it was expedient to have as few objections as possible to the proposed scheme of government, he thought it best to leave the matter as we find it. He observed that the abolition of slavery seemed to be going on in the United States, and that the good sense of the several states would probably by degrees complete it. He urged on the Convention the necessity of despatching its business.

MR. MASON. This infernal traffic originated in the avarice of British Merchants. The British government constantly checked the attempts of Virginia to put a stop to it. The present question concerns not the importing states alone but the whole Union. The evil of having slaves was experienced during the late war. Had slaves been treated as they might have been by the enemy, they would have proved dangerous instruments in their hands. But their folly dealt by the slaves, as it did by the Tories. He mentioned the dangerous insurrections of the slaves in Greece and Sicily; and the instructions given by Cromwell to the commissioners sent to Virginia to arm the servants and slaves, in case other means of obtaining its submission should fail. Maryland and Virginia, he said, had already prohibited the importation of slaves expressly. North Carolina had done the same in substance. All this would be in vain if South Carolina and Georgia be at liberty to import. The Western people are already calling out for slaves for their new lands, and will fill that country with slaves if they can be got through South Carolina and Georgia. Slavery discourages arts and manufactures. The poor despise labor when performed by slaves. They prevent the immigration of Whites, who really enrich and strengthen a country. They produce the most pernicious effect on manners. Every master of slaves is born a petty tyrant. They bring the judgment of heaven on a country. As nations can not be rewarded or punished in the next world they must be in this. By an inevitable chain of causes and effects providence punishes national sins by national calamities. He lamented that some of our Eastern brethren had from a lust of gain embarked in this nefarious traffic. As to the states being in possession of the right to import, this was the case with many other rights, now to be properly given up. He held it essential in every point of view that the general government should have power to prevent the increase of slavery.

MR. ELLSWORTH, as he had never owned a slave, could not judge of the effects of slavery on character. He said, however, that if it was to be considered in a moral light, we ought to go further and free those already in the country. As slaves also multiply so fast in Virginia and Maryland that it is cheaper to raise than import them, whilst in the sickly rice-swamps foreign supplies are necessary; if we go no further than is urged, we shall be unjust towards South Carolina and Georgia. Let us not intermeddle. As population increases, poor laborers will be so plenty as to render slaves useless. *Slavery, in time, will not be a speck in our country.* Provision is already made in Connecticut for abolishing it; and the abolition has already taken place in Massachusetts. As to the danger of insurrections from foreign influence, that will become a motive to kind treatment of the slaves.

Mr. [CHARLES] PINCKNEY. If slavery be wrong, it is justified by the example of all the world. He cited the case of Greece, Rome, and other ancient states, the sanction given by France, England, Holland and other modern states. In all ages one half of mankind have been slaves. If the Southern states were let alone, they will probably of themselves stop importations. He would himself, as a citizen of South Carolina, vote for it. An attempt to take away the right, as proposed, will produce serious objections to the Constitution, which he wished to see adopted.

GEN. [CHARLES COTESWORTH] PINCKNEY declared it to be his firm opinion that if himself and all his colleagues were to sign the Constitution, and use their personal influence, it would be of no avail towards obtaining the assent of their constituents. South Carolina and Georgia cannot do without slaves. As to Virginia, she will gain by stopping the importations. Her slaves will rise in value, and she has more than she wants. It would be unequal to require South Carolina and Georgia to confederate on such unequal terms. He said, the royal assent, before the Revolution, had never been refused to South Carolina as to Virginia. He contended that the importation of slaves would be for the interest of the whole Union. The more slaves, the more produce to employ the carrying-trade; the more consumption also: and, the more of this, the more revenue for the common treasury. He admitted it to be reasonable that slaves should be dutied like other imports; but should consider a rejection of the clause as an exclusion of South Carolina from the Union.

Mr. BALDWIN had conceived national objects alone to be before the Convention; not such as, like the present, were of a local nature. Georgia was decided on this point. That state has always hitherto supposed a general government to be the pursuit of the central states, who wished to have a vortex for everything; that her distance would preclude her, from equal advantage; and that she could not prudently purchase it by yielding national powers. From this it might be understood in what light she would view an attempt to abridge one of her favorite prerogatives. If left to herself, she may probably put a stop to the evil. As one ground for this conjecture, he took notice of the sect of _____, which he said was a respectable class of people, who carried their ethics beyond the mere *equality of men,* extending their humanity to the claims of the whole animal creation.

MR. WILSON observed that if South Carolina and Georgia were themselves disposed to get rid of the importation of slaves in a short time, as had been suggested, they would never refuse to unite because the importation might be prohibited. As the section now stands, all articles imported are to be taxed. Slaves alone are exempt. This is in fact a bounty on that article.

MR. GERRY thought we had nothing to do with the conduct of the states as to slaves, but ought to be careful not to give any sanction to it.

MR. DICKINSON considered it as inadmissible, on every principle of honor and safety, that the importation of slaves should be authorized to the states by the Constitution. The true question was, whether the national happiness would be promoted or impeded by the importation; and this question ought to be left to the national government, not to the states particularly interested. If England and France permit slavery, slaves are, at the same time, excluded from both those kingdoms. Greece and Rome were made unhappy by their slaves. He could not believe that the Southern states would refuse to confederate on the account apprehended; especially as the power was not likely to be immediately exercised by the general government.

MR. WILLIAMSON stated the law of North Carolina on the subject, to wit, that it did not directly prohibit the importation of slaves. It imposed a duty of £5 on each slave imported from Africa; £10 on each from elsewhere; and £50 on each from a state licensing manumission. He thought the Southern states could not be members of the Union, if the clause should be rejected; and that it was wrong to force anything down not absolutely necessary, and which any state must disagree to.

MR. KING thought the subject should be considered in a political light only. If two states will not agree to the Constitution, as stated on one side, he could affirm with equal belief, on the other, that great and equal opposition would be experienced from the other states. He remarked on the exemption of slaves from duty, whilst every other import was subjected to it, as an inequality that could not fail to strike the commercial sagacity of the Northern and Middle states.

MR. LANGDON was strenuous for giving the power to the general government. He could not, with a good conscience, leave it with the states, who could then go on with the traffic, without being restrained by the opinions here given, that they will themselves cease to import slaves.

GENERAL PINCKNEY thought himself bound to declare candidly that he did not think South Carolina would stop her importations of slaves, in any short time; but only stop them occasionally as she now does. He moved to commit the clause that slaves might be made liable to an equal tax with other imports, which he thought right, and which would remove one difficulty that had been started.

MR. RUTLEDGE. If the Convention thinks that North Carolina, South Carolina, and Georgia, will ever agree to the plan, unless their right to import slaves be untouched, the expectation is vain. The people of those states will never be such fools as to give up so important an interest. He was strenuous against striking out the section, and seconded the motion of General Pinckney for a commitment.

MR. GOUVERNEUR MORRIS wished the whole subject to be committed, including the clauses relating to taxes on exports and to a navigation act. These things may form a bargain among the Northern and Southern states.

MR. BUTLER declared that he never would agree to the power taxing exports.

MR. SHERMAN said it was better to let the Southern states import slaves than to part with them, if they made that a *sine qua non*. He was opposed to a tax on slaves imported, as making the matter worse, because it implied they were *property*. He acknowledged that if the power of prohibiting the importation should be given to the general government, that it would be exercised. He thought it would be its duty to exercise the power.

MR. READ was for the commitment, provided the clause concerning taxes on exports should also be committed.

MR. SHERMAN observed that that clause had been agreed to, and therefore could not be committed. .

MR. RANDOLPH was for committing, in order that some middle ground might, if possible, be found. He could never agree to the clause as it stands. He would sooner risk the Constitution. He dwelt on the dilemma to which the convention was exposed. By agreeing to the clause, it would revolt the Quakers, the Methodists, and many others in states having no slaves. On the other hand, two states might be lost to the union. Let us then, he said, try the chance of a commitment.

On the question for committing the remaining part of Sections 4 and 5, of Article 7,—Connecticut, New Jersey, Maryland, Virginia, North Carolina, South Carolina, Georgia, *aye*—seven; New Hampshire, Pennsylvania, Delaware, *no*—eight; Massachusetts absent.

DEBATE ON AMENDMENTS TO THE CONSTITUTION IN THE FEDERAL CONVENTION: ELBRIDGE GERRY, ALEXANDER HAMILTON, JAMES MADISON, EDMUND RANDOLPH, AND OTHERS

("The national legislature will be the first to perceive and will be most sensible to the necessity of amendments, and ought also to be empowered whenever two thirds of each branch should concur to call a convention")

FEDERAL CONVENTION, PHILADELPHIA
SEPTEMBER 10, 1787

> *The lack of a Bill of Rights would become one of the major stumbling blocks in the ratification of the Constitution. To go back, however, after months of painstaking negotiations on the Constitution and try to find consensus on a Bill of Rights was, believed James Madison, hopeless and would sink the Constitution in the process. The obvious impending need for amendments to the Constitution was, on the other hand, an important point to be clarified. (As settled in Article 5 of the Constitution:* "The Congress, whenever two thirds of both Houses shall deem it necessary, shall propose Amendments to this Constitution, or, on the Application of the Legislatures of two thirds of the several States, shall call a Convention for proposing Amendments, which, in either Case, shall be valid to all Intents and Purposes, as Part of this Constitution, when ratified by the Legislatures of three fourths of the several States, or by Conventions in three fourths thereof, as the one or the other Mode of Ratification may be proposed by the Congress ..." *)*

MR. GERRY moved to reconsider Article 19, namely, "On the application of the legislatures of two thirds of the states in the union, for an amendment of this Constitution, the legislature of the U.S. shall call a convention for that purpose." This Constitution, he said, is to be paramount to the state constitutions. It follows, hence, from this article that two thirds of the states may obtain a convention, a majority of which can bind the union to innovations that may subvert the state-constitutions altogether. He asked whether this was a situation proper to be run into.

MR. HAMILTON seconded the motion, but he said with a different view from Mr. Gerry. He did not object to the consequence stated by Mr. Gerry. There was no greater evil in subjecting the people of the United States to the major voice than the people of a particular state. It had been wished by many and was much to have been desired that an easier mode for introducing amendments had been provided by the Articles of Confederation. It was equally desirable now that an easy mode should be established for supplying defects which will probably appear in the new system. The mode proposed was not adequate. The state legislatures will not apply for alterations but with a view to increase their own powers. The national legislature will be the first to perceive and will be most sensible to the necessity of amendments, and ought also to be empowered whenever two thirds of each branch should concur to call a convention. There could be no danger in giving this power, as the people would finally decide in the case.

MR. MADISON remarked on the vagueness of the terms, "call a convention for the purpose," as sufficient reason for reconsidering the article. How was a convention to be formed? By what rule decide? What the force of its acts?

On the motion of MR. GERRY to reconsider:

Massachusetts, Connecticut, Pennsylvania, Delaware, Maryland, Virginia, North Carolina, South Carolina, Georgia, *aye*—nine; New Jersey, *no*—one; New Hampshire, *divided*.

MR. SHERMAN moved to add to the article "or the legislature may propose amendments to the several states for their approbation, but no amendments shall be binding until consented to by the several states."

MR. GERRY seconded the motion.

MR. WILSON moved to insert "two thirds of" before the words "several states," on which amendment to the motion of Mr. Sherman:

New Hampshire, Pennsylvania, Delaware, Maryland, Virginia, *aye*—five; Massachusetts, Connecticut, New Jersey, North Carolina, South Carolina, Georgia, *no*—six.

MR. WILSON then moved to insert "three fourths of" before "the several states," which was agreed to unanimously.

MR. MADISON moved to postpone the consideration of the amended proposition in order to take up the following,

"The legislature of the United States, whenever two thirds of both houses shall deem necessary, or on the application of two thirds of the legislatures of the several states, shall propose amendments to this Constitution, which shall be valid to all intents and purposes as part thereof, when the same shall have been ratified by three fourths at least of the legislatures of the several states, or by conventions in three fourths thereof, as one or the other mode of ratification may be proposed by the legislature of the United States."

Mr. Hamilton seconded the motion.

Mr. Rutledge said he never could agree to give a power by which the articles relating to slaves might be altered by the states not interested in that property and prejudiced against it. In order to obviate this objection, these words were added to the proposition: "provided that no amendments which may be made prior to the year 1808, shall in any manner affect the fourth and fifth sections of the seventh article."

The postponement being agreed to, on the question on the proposition of Mr. Madison and Mr. Hamilton as amended:

Massachusetts, Connecticut, New Jersey, Pennsylvania, Maryland, Virginia, North Carolina, South Carolina, Georgia, *aye*—nine; Delaware, *no*—one; New Hampshire, *divided*.

Mr. Gerry moved to reconsider Articles 21 and 22 from the latter of which "for the approbation of Congress" had been struck out. He objected to proceeding to change the government without the approbation of Congress, as being improper and giving just umbrage to that body. He repeated his objections also to an annulment of the confederation with so little scruple or formality.

Mr. Hamilton concurred with Mr. Gerry as to the indecorum of not requiring the approbation of Congress. He considered this as a necessary ingredient in the transaction. He thought it wrong also to allow nine states as provided by Article 21 to institute a new government on the ruins of the existing one. He would propose as a better modification of the two articles (21 and 22) that the plan should be sent to Congress in order that the same, if approved by them, may be communicated to the state legislatures, to the end that they may refer it to state conventions; each legislature declaring that if the convention of the state should think the plan ought to take effect among nine ratifying states, the same should take effect accordingly.

Mr. Gorham. Some states will say that nine states shall be sufficient to establish the plan, others will require unanimity for the purpose. And the different and conditional ratifications will defeat the plan altogether.

Mr. Hamilton. No convention convinced of the necessity of the plan will refuse to give it effect on the adoption by nine states. He thought this mode less exceptionable than the one proposed in the article, and would attain the same end.

MR. FITZSIMMONS remarked that the words "for their approbation" had been struck out in order to save Congress from the necessity of an act inconsistent with the Articles of Confederation under which they held their authority.

MR. RANDOLPH declared, if no change should be made in this part of the plan, he should be obliged to dissent from the whole of it. He had from the beginning he said been convinced that radical changes in the system of the union were necessary. Under this conviction he had brought forward a set of republican propositions as the basis and outline of a reform. These republican propositions had, however, much to his regret, been widely and in his opinion irreconcilably departed from. In this state of things it was his idea and he accordingly meant to propose that the state conventions should be at liberty to offer amendments to the plan; and that these should be submitted to a second general convention, with full power to settle the Constitution finally. He did not expect to succeed in this proposition, but the discharge of his duty in making the attempt would give quiet to his own mind.

MR. WILSON was against a reconsideration for any of the purposes which had been mentioned.

MR. KING thought it would be more respectful to Congress to submit the plan generally to them than in such a form as expressly and necessarily to require their approbation or disapprobation. The assent of nine states be considered as sufficient; and that it was more proper to make this a part of the Constitution itself than to provide for it by a supplemental or distinct recommendation.

MR. GERRY urged the indecency and pernicious tendency of dissolving in so slight a manner the solemn obligations of the Articles of Confederation. If nine out of thirteen can dissolve the compact, six out of nine will be just as able to dissolve the new one hereafter.

MR. SHERMAN was in favor of Mr. King's idea of submitting the plan generally to Congress. He thought nine states ought to be made sufficient: but that it would be best to make it a separate act and in some such form as that intimated by Colonel Hamilton than to make it a particular article of the Constitution.

On the question for reconsidering the Articles 21 and 22:

Connecticut, New Jersey, Delaware, Maryland, Virginia, North Carolina, Georgia, *aye*—seven; Massachusetts, Pennsylvania, South Carolina, *no*—three; New Hampshire, *divided*.

MR. HAMILTON then moved to postpone Article 21 in order to take up the following, containing the ideas he had above expressed, namely:

"Resolved that the foregoing plan of a Constitution be transmitted to the United States in Congress assembled, in order that if the same shall be agreed to by them, it may be communicated to the legislatures of the several states, to the end that they may provide for its final ratification by referring the same to the consideration of a convention of deputies in each state to be chosen by the people thereof, and that it be recommended to the said legislatures in their respective acts for organizing such convention to declare, that if the said convention shall approve of the said Constitution, such approbation shall be binding and conclusive upon the state, and further that if the said convention should be of opinion that the same upon the assent of any nine states thereto, ought to take effect between the states so assenting, such opinion shall thereupon be also binding upon such state, and the said Constitution shall take effect between the states assenting thereto."

Mr. Gerry seconded the motion.

Mr. Wilson. This motion being seconded, it is necessary now to speak freely. He expressed in strong terms his disapprobation of the expedient proposed, particularly the suspending the plan of the convention on the approbation of Congress. He declared it to be worse than folly to rely on the concurrence of the Rhode Island members of Congress in the plan. Maryland has voted on this floor for requiring the unanimous assent of the thirteen states to the proposed change in the federal system. New York has not been represented for a long time past in the convention. Many individual deputies from other states have spoken much against the plan. Under these circumstances can it be safe to make the assent of Congress necessary? After spending four or five months in the laborious and arduous task of forming a government for our country, we are ourselves at the close throwing insuperable obstacles in the way of its success.

Mr. Clymer thought that the mode proposed by Mr. Hamilton would fetter and embarrass Congress as much as the original one, since it equally involved a breach of the Articles of Confederation.

Mr. King concurred with Mr. Clymer. If Congress can accede to one mode, they can to the other. If the approbation of Congress be made necessary, and they should not approve, the state legislatures will not propose the plan to conventions; or if the states themselves are to provide that nine states shall suffice to establish the system, that provision will be omitted, everything will go into confusion, and all our labor be lost.

Mr. Rutledge viewed the matter in the same light with Mr. King. On the question to postpone in order to take up Colonel Hamilton's motion:

Connecticut, *aye*—one; New Hampshire, Massachusetts, New Jersey, Pennsylvania, Delaware, Maryland, Virginia, North Carolina, South Carolina, Georiga, *no*—ten.

A question being then taken on the Article 21. It was agreed to unanimously.

MR. HAMILTON withdrew the remainder of the motion to postpone Article 22, observing that his purpose was defeated by the vote just given.

MR. WILLIAMSON and Mr. GERRY moved to reinstate the words "for the approbation of Congress" in Article 22, which was disagreed to unanimously.

MR. RANDOLPH took this opportunity to state his objections to the system. They turned on the senate's being made the court of impeachment for trying the executive; on the necessity of three-fourths instead of two-thirds of each house to overrule the negative of the President; on the smallness of the number of the representative branch; on the want of limitation to a standing army; on the general clause concerning necessary and proper laws; on the want of some particular restraint on navigation acts; on the power to lay duties on exports; on the authority of the general legislature to interpose on the application of the executives of the states; on the want of a more definite boundary between the general and state legislatures; and between the general and state judiciaries; on the unqualified power of the President to pardon treasons; on the want of some limit to the power of the legislature in regulating their own compensations.

With these difficulties in his mind, what course—he asked—was he to pursue? Was he to promote the establishment of a plan which he verily believed would end in tyranny? He was unwilling, he said, to impede the wishes and judgment of the convention, but he must keep himself free, in case he should be honored with a seat in the convention of his state, to act according to the dictates of his judgment. The only mode in which his embarrassments could be removed was that of submitting the plan to Congress to go from them to the state legislatures, and from these to state conventions having power to adopt, reject or amend; the process to close with another general convention with full power to adopt or reject the alterations proposed by the state conventions, and to establish finally the government. He accordingly proposed a resolution to this effect.

DR. FRANKLIN seconded the motion.

MR. MASON urged and obtained that the motion should lie on the table for a day or two to see what steps might be taken with regard to the parts of the system objected to by Mr. Randolph.

MR. PINCKNEY moved "that it be an instruction to the committee for revising the style and arrangement of the articles agreed on, to prepare an address to the people, to accompany the present Constitution, and to be laid with the same before the United States in Congress."

The motion itself was referred to the committee unanimously.

MR. RANDOLPH moved to refer to the committee also a motion relating to pardons in cases of treason, which was agreed to unanimously.

Adjourned.

ADDRESS TO THE CONSTITUTIONAL
CONVENTION BY BENJAMIN FRANKLIN

("Thus I consent, sir, to this Constitution because I expect no
better, and because I am not sure that it is not the best")

FEDERAL CONVENTION, PHILADELPHIA
SEPTEMBER 17, 1787

> *Benjamin Franklin (1706–1790) and George Washington (1732–
> 1799) were the two most famous men in America, recognized for
> their wisdom and leadership. On this, the final day of the Federal
> Convention, Franklin, apparently in ill health, asked his fellow
> Pennsylvania delegate James Wilson to read aloud these words for
> him to the convention. Three delegates, in spite of Franklin's plea for
> unanimity, refused to sign.*

Mr. President,

I confess that there are several parts of this constitution which I
do not at present approve, but I am not sure I shall never approve
them: For having lived long, I have experienced many instances of being obliged by better information, or fuller consideration, to change
opinions even on important subjects, which I once thought right, but
found to be otherwise. It is therefore that the older I grow, the more
apt I am to doubt my own judgment, and to pay more respect to the
judgment of others. Most men indeed, as well as most sects in religion,
think themselves in possession of all truth, and that wherever others
differ from them it is so far error. Steele, a Protestant, in a dedication
tells the Pope that the only difference between our churches in their
opinions of the certainty of their doctrines is, the Church of Rome
is infallible and the Church of England is never in the wrong. But
though many private persons think almost as highly of their own infallibility as of that of their sect, few express it so naturally as a certain
French lady, who in a dispute with her sister, said, "I don't know how

it happens, sister, but I meet with nobody but myself that's always in the right.— *Il n'y a que moi qui a toujours raison.*"

In these sentiments, sir, I agree to this Constitution with all its faults, if they are such; because I think a general government necessary for us, and there is no form of government but what may be a blessing to the people if well administered, and believe farther that this is likely to be well administered for a course of years, and can only end in despotism, as other forms have done before it, when the people shall become so corrupted as to need despotic government, being incapable of any other. I doubt too whether any other convention we can obtain may be able to make a better Constitution. For when you assemble a number of men to have the advantage of their joint wisdom, you inevitably assemble with those men all their prejudices, their passions, their errors of opinion, their local interests, and their selfish views. From such an assembly, can a perfect production be expected? It therefore astonishes me, sir, to find this system approaching so near to perfection as it does; and I think it will astonish our enemies, who are waiting with confidence to hear that our councils are confounded like those of the builders of Babel; and that our states are on the point of separation, only to meet hereafter for the purpose of cutting one another's throats. Thus I consent, sir, to this Constitution because I expect no better, and because I am not sure that it is not the best. The opinions I have had of its errors, I sacrifice to the public good. I have never whispered a syllable of them abroad. Within these walls they were born, and here they shall die. If every one of us in returning to our constituents were to report the objections he has had to it, and endeavor to gain partisans in support of them, we might prevent its being generally received, and thereby lose all the salutary effects and great advantages resulting naturally in our favor among foreign nations as well as among ourselves from our real or apparent unanimity. Much of the strength and efficiency of any government in procuring and securing happiness to the people, depends on opinion, on the general opinion of the goodness of the government, as well as of the wisdom and integrity of its governors. I hope therefore that for our own sakes as a part of the people, and for the sake of posterity, we shall act heartily and unanimously in recommending this Constitution (if approved by Congress and confirmed by the conventions) wherever our influence may extend, and turn our future thoughts and endeavors to the means of having it well administered.

On the whole, sir, I can not help expressing a wish that every member of the convention who may still have objections to it, would with me, on this occasion, doubt a little of his own infallibility, and to make manifest our unanimity, put his name to this instrument.

LETTER OF THE PRESIDENT OF THE FEDERAL CONVENTION, GEORGE WASHINGTON, TO THE PRESIDENT OF CONGRESS, TRANSMITTING THE CONSTITUTION

("... the Constitution, which we now present, is the result of a spirit of amity, and of that mutual deference and concession which the peculiarity of our political situation rendered indispensable")

FEDERAL CONVENTION, PHILADELPHIA
SEPTEMBER 17, 1787

George Washington, fifty-five years old, respected and revered by all, the president of this Convention and soon to be the president of this country, was the formal presenter of the Constitution.

Sir,

We have now the honor to submit to the consideration of the United States in Congress assembled, that Constitution which has appeared to us the most advisable.

The friends of our country have long seen and desired, that the power of making war, peace, and treaties, that of levying money and regulating commerce, and the correspondent executive and judicial authorities should be fully and effectually vested in the general government of the Union: But the impropriety of delegating such extensive trust to one body of men is evident—Hence results the necessity of a different organization.

It is obviously impracticable in the federal government of these states, to secure all rights of independent sovereignty to each, and yet provide for the interest and safety of all: Individuals entering into society, must give up a share of liberty to preserve the rest. The magnitude of the sacrifice must depend as well on situation and circumstance, as on the object to be obtained. It is at all times difficult to draw with precision the line between those rights which must be surrendered, and those which may be reserved; and on the present occasion this difficulty was increased by a difference among the several states as to their situation, extent, habits, and particular interests.

In all our deliberations on this subject we kept steadily in our view, that which appears to us the greatest interest of every true American, the consolidation of our Union, in which is involved our prosperity, felicity, safety, perhaps our national existence. This important consideration, seriously and deeply impressed on our minds, led each state in the Convention to be less rigid on points of inferior magnitude, than might have been otherwise expected; and thus the Constitution, which we now present, is the result of a spirit of amity, and of that mutual deference and concession which the peculiarity of our political situation rendered indispensable.

That it will meet the full and entire approbation of every state is not perhaps to be expected; but each will doubtless consider, that had her interest been alone consulted, the consequences might have been particularly disagreeable or injurious to others; that it is liable to as few exceptions as could reasonably have been expected, we hope and believe; that it may promote the lasting welfare of that country so dear to us all, and secure her freedom and happiness, is our most ardent wish.

With great respect,
We have the honor to be, Sir,
Your Excellency's most obedient and humble servants,
GEORGE WASHINGTON, President.
By unanimous Order of the Convention.
His Excellency the PRESIDENT of CONGRESS.

THE CONSTITUTION OF THE UNITED STATES OF AMERICA

SEPTEMBER 17, 1787

We the People of the United States, in Order to form a more perfect Union, establish Justice, insure domestic Tranquility, provide for the common defence, promote the general Welfare, and secure the Blessings of Liberty to ourselves and our Posterity, do ordain and establish this Constitution for the United States of America.

Article. I.

Section. 1.

All legislative Powers herein granted shall be vested in a Congress of the United States, which shall consist of a Senate and House of Representatives.

Section. 2.

The House of Representatives shall be composed of Members chosen every second Year by the People of the several States, and the Electors in each State shall have the Qualifications requisite for Electors of the most numerous Branch of the State Legislature.

No Person shall be a Representative who shall not have attained to the Age of twenty five Years, and been seven Years a Citizen of the United States, and who shall not, when elected, be an Inhabitant of that State in which he shall be chosen.

Representatives and direct Taxes shall be apportioned among the several States which may be included within this Union, according to their respective Numbers, which shall be determined by adding to the whole Number of free Persons, including those bound to Service for a Term of Years, and excluding Indians not taxed, three fifths of all other Persons. The actual Enumeration shall be made within three Years after the first Meeting of the Congress of the United States, and within every subsequent Term of ten Years, in such Manner as they shall by Law direct. The Number of Representatives shall not exceed one for every thirty Thousand, but each State shall have at Least one Representative; and until such enumeration shall be made, the State of New Hampshire shall be entitled to chuse three, Massachusetts eight, Rhode-Island and Providence Plantations one, Connecticut five, New-York six, New Jersey four, Pennsylvania eight, Delaware one, Maryland six, Virginia ten, North Carolina five, South Carolina five, and Georgia three.

When vacancies happen in the Representation from any State, the Executive Authority thereof shall issue Writs of Election to fill such Vacancies.

The House of Representatives shall chuse their Speaker and other Officers; and shall have the sole Power of Impeachment.

Section. 3.

The Senate of the United States shall be composed of two Senators from each State, chosen by the Legislature thereof for six Years; and each Senator shall have one Vote.

Immediately after they shall be assembled in Consequence of the first Election, they shall be divided as equally as may be into three Classes. The Seats of the Senators of the first Class shall be vacated at the Expiration of the second Year, of the second Class at the Expiration of the fourth Year, and of the third Class at the Expiration of the sixth Year, so that one third may be chosen every second Year; and if Vacancies happen by Resignation, or otherwise, during the Recess of the Legislature of any State, the Executive thereof may make temporary Appointments until the next Meeting of the Legislature, which shall then fill such Vacancies.

No Person shall be a Senator who shall not have attained to the Age of thirty Years, and been nine Years a Citizen of the United States, and who shall not, when elected, be an Inhabitant of that State for which he shall be chosen.

The Vice President of the United States shall be President of the Senate, but shall have no Vote, unless they be equally divided.

The Senate shall chuse their other Officers, and also a President pro tempore, in the Absence of the Vice President, or when he shall exercise the Office of President of the United States.

The Senate shall have the sole Power to try all Impeachments. When sitting for that Purpose, they shall be on Oath or Affirmation. When the President of the United States is tried, the Chief Justice shall preside: And no Person shall be convicted without the Concurrence of two thirds of the Members present.

Judgment in Cases of Impeachment shall not extend further than to removal from Office, and disqualification to hold and enjoy any

Office of honor, Trust or Profit under the United States: but the Party convicted shall nevertheless be liable and subject to Indictment, Trial, Judgment and Punishment, according to Law.

Section. 4.

The Times, Places and Manner of holding Elections for Senators and Representatives, shall be prescribed in each State by the Legislature thereof; but the Congress may at any time by Law make or alter such Regulations, except as to the Places of chusing Senators.

The Congress shall assemble at least once in every Year, and such Meeting shall be on the first Monday in December, unless they shall by Law appoint a different Day.

Section. 5.

Each House shall be the Judge of the Elections, Returns and Qualifications of its own Members, and a Majority of each shall constitute a Quorum to do Business; but a smaller Number may adjourn from day to day, and may be authorized to compel the Attendance of absent Members, in such Manner, and under such Penalties as each House may provide.

Each House may determine the Rules of its Proceedings, punish its Members for disorderly Behaviour, and, with the Concurrence of two thirds, expel a Member.

Each House shall keep a Journal of its Proceedings, and from time to time publish the same, excepting such Parts as may in their Judgment require Secrecy; and the Yeas and Nays of the Members of either House on any question shall, at the Desire of one fifth of those Present, be entered on the Journal.

Neither House, during the Session of Congress, shall, without the Consent of the other, adjourn for more than three days, nor to any other Place than that in which the two Houses shall be sitting.

Section. 6.

The Senators and Representatives shall receive a Compensation for their Services, to be ascertained by Law, and paid out of the Treasury of the United States. They shall in all Cases, except Treason, Felony and Breach of the Peace, be privileged from Arrest during their Attendance at the Session of their respective Houses, and in going to and returning from the same; and for any Speech or Debate in either House, they shall not be questioned in any other Place.

No Senator or Representative shall, during the Time for which he was elected, be appointed to any civil Office under the Authority of the United States, which shall have been created, or the Emoluments whereof shall have been encreased during such time; and no Person holding any Office under the United States, shall be a Member of either House during his Continuance in Office.

Section. 7.

All Bills for raising Revenue shall originate in the House of Representatives; but the Senate may propose or concur with Amendments as on other Bills.

Every Bill which shall have passed the House of Representatives and the Senate, shall, before it become a Law, be presented to the President of the United States: If he approve he shall sign it, but if not he shall return it, with his Objections to that House in which it shall have originated, who shall enter the Objections at large on their Journal, and proceed to reconsider it. If after such Reconsideration two thirds of that House shall agree to pass the Bill, it shall be sent, together with the Objections, to the other House, by which it shall likewise be reconsidered, and if approved by two thirds of that House, it shall become a Law. But in all such Cases the Votes of both Houses shall be determined by yeas and Nays, and the Names of the Persons voting for and against the Bill shall be entered on the Journal of each House respectively. If any Bill shall not be returned by the President within ten Days (Sundays excepted) after it shall have been presented to him, the Same shall be a Law, in like Manner as if he had signed it, unless the Congress by their Adjournment prevent its Return, in which Case it shall not be a Law.

Every Order, Resolution, or Vote to which the Concurrence of the Senate and House of Representatives may be necessary (except on a question of Adjournment) shall be presented to the President of the United States; and before the Same shall take Effect, shall be approved by him, or being disapproved by him, shall be repassed by two thirds of the Senate and House of Representatives, according to the Rules and Limitations prescribed in the Case of a Bill.

Section. 8.

The Congress shall have Power To lay and collect Taxes, Duties, Imposts and Excises, to pay the Debts and provide for the common Defence and general Welfare of the United States; but all Duties, Imposts and Excises shall be uniform throughout the United States;

To borrow Money on the credit of the United States;

To regulate Commerce with foreign Nations, and among the several States, and with the Indian Tribes;

To establish an uniform Rule of Naturalization, and uniform Laws on the subject of Bankruptcies throughout the United States;

To coin Money, regulate the Value thereof, and of foreign Coin, and fix the Standard of Weights and Measures;

To provide for the Punishment of counterfeiting the Securities and current Coin of the United States;

To establish Post Offices and post Roads;

To promote the Progress of Science and useful Arts, by securing for limited Times to Authors and Inventors the exclusive Right to their respective Writings and Discoveries;

To constitute Tribunals inferior to the supreme Court;

To define and punish Piracies and Felonies committed on the high Seas, and Offences against the Law of Nations;

To declare War, grant Letters of Marque and Reprisal, and make Rules concerning Captures on Land and Water;

To raise and support Armies, but no Appropriation of Money to that Use shall be for a longer Term than two Years;

To provide and maintain a Navy;

To make Rules for the Government and Regulation of the land and naval Forces;

To provide for calling forth the Militia to execute the Laws of the Union, suppress Insurrections and repel Invasions;

To provide for organizing, arming, and disciplining, the Militia, and for governing such Part of them as may be employed in the Service of the United States, reserving to the States respectively, the Appointment of the Officers, and the Authority of training the Militia according to the discipline prescribed by Congress;

To exercise exclusive Legislation in all Cases whatsoever, over such District (not exceeding ten Miles square) as may, by Cession of particular States, and the Acceptance of Congress, become the Seat of the Government of the United States, and to exercise like Authority over all Places purchased by the Consent of the Legislature of the State in which the Same shall be, for the Erection of Forts, Magazines, Arsenals, dock-Yards, and other needful Buildings;—And

To make all Laws which shall be necessary and proper for carrying into Execution the foregoing Powers, and all other Powers vested by this Constitution in the Government of the United States, or in any Department or Officer thereof.

Section. 9.

The Migration or Importation of such Persons as any of the States now existing shall think proper to admit, shall not be prohibited by the Congress prior to the Year one thousand eight hundred and eight, but a Tax or duty may be imposed on such Importation, not exceeding ten dollars for each Person.

The Privilege of the Writ of Habeas Corpus shall not be suspended, unless when in Cases of Rebellion or Invasion the public Safety may require it.

No Bill of Attainder or ex post facto Law shall be passed.

No Capitation, or other direct, Tax shall be laid, unless in Proportion to the Census or enumeration herein before directed to be taken.

No Tax or Duty shall be laid on Articles exported from any State.

No Preference shall be given by any Regulation of Commerce or Revenue to the Ports of one State over those of another; nor shall Vessels bound to, or from, one State, be obliged to enter, clear, or pay Duties in another.

No Money shall be drawn from the Treasury, but in Consequence of Appropriations made by Law; and a regular Statement and Account of the Receipts and Expenditures of all public Money shall be published from time to time.

No Title of Nobility shall be granted by the United States: And no Person holding any Office of Profit or Trust under them, shall, without the Consent of the Congress, accept of any present, Emolument, Office, or Title, of any kind whatever, from any King, Prince, or foreign State.

Section. 10.

No State shall enter into any Treaty, Alliance, or Confederation; grant Letters of Marque and Reprisal; coin Money; emit Bills of Credit; make any Thing but gold and silver Coin a Tender in Payment of Debts; pass any Bill of Attainder, ex post facto Law, or Law impairing the Obligation of Contracts, or grant any Title of Nobility.

No State shall, without the Consent of the Congress, lay any Imposts or Duties on Imports or Exports, except what may be absolutely necessary for executing it's inspection Laws: and the net Produce of all Duties and Imposts, laid by any State on Imports or Exports, shall be for the Use of the Treasury of the United States; and all such Laws shall be subject to the Revision and Controul of the Congress.

No State shall, without the Consent of Congress, lay any Duty of Tonnage, keep Troops, or Ships of War in time of Peace, enter into any Agreement or Compact with another State, or with a foreign Power, or engage in War, unless actually invaded, or in such imminent Danger as will not admit of delay.

Article. II.

Section. 1.

The executive Power shall be vested in a President of the United States of America. He shall hold his Office during the Term of four Years, and, together with the Vice President, chosen for the same Term, be elected, as follows:

Each State shall appoint, in such Manner as the Legislature thereof may direct, a Number of Electors, equal to the whole Number of Senators and Representatives to which the State may be entitled in the Congress: but no Senator or Representative, or Person holding an Office of Trust or Profit under the United States, shall be appointed an Elector.

The Electors shall meet in their respective States, and vote by Ballot for two Persons, of whom one at least shall not be an Inhabitant of the same State with themselves. And they shall make a List of all the Persons voted for, and of the Number of Votes for each; which List they shall sign and certify, and transmit sealed to the Seat of the Government of the United States, directed to the President of the Senate. The President of the Senate shall, in the Presence of the Senate and House of Representatives, open all the Certificates, and the Votes shall then be counted. The Person having the greatest Number of Votes shall be the President, if such Number be a Majority of the whole Number of Electors appointed; and if there be more than one who have such Majority, and have an equal Number of Votes, then the House of Representatives shall immediately chuse by Ballot one of them for President; and if no Person have a Majority, then from the five highest on the List the said House shall in like Manner chuse the President. But in chusing the President, the Votes shall be taken by States, the Representation from each State having one Vote; a quorum for this purpose shall consist of a Member or Members from two thirds of the States, and a Majority of all the States shall be necessary to a Choice. In every Case, after the Choice of the President, the Person having the greatest Number of Votes of the Electors shall be the Vice President. But if there should remain two or more who have equal Votes, the Senate shall chuse from them by Ballot the Vice President.

The Congress may determine the Time of chusing the Electors, and the Day on which they shall give their Votes; which Day shall be the same throughout the United States.

No Person except a natural born Citizen, or a Citizen of the United States, at the time of the Adoption of this Constitution, shall be eligible to the Office of President; neither shall any Person be eligible to that Office who shall not have attained to the Age of thirty five Years, and been fourteen Years a Resident within the United States.

In Case of the Removal of the President from Office, or of his Death, Resignation, or Inability to discharge the Powers and Duties of the said Office, the Same shall devolve on the Vice President, and the Congress may by Law provide for the Case of Removal, Death, Resignation or Inability, both of the President and Vice President, declaring what Officer shall then act as President, and such Officer shall act accordingly, until the Disability be removed, or a President shall be elected.

The President shall, at stated Times, receive for his Services, a Compensation, which shall neither be increased nor diminished during the Period for which he shall have been elected, and he shall not receive within that Period any other Emolument from the United States, or any of them.

Before he enter on the Execution of his Office, he shall take the following Oath or Affirmation:—"I do solemnly swear (or affirm) that I will faithfully execute the Office of President of the United States, and will to the best of my Ability, preserve, protect and defend the Constitution of the United States."

Section. 2.

The President shall be Commander in Chief of the Army and Navy of the United States, and of the Militia of the several States, when called into the actual Service of the United States; he may require the Opinion, in writing, of the principal Officer in each of the executive Departments, upon any Subject relating to the Duties of their respective Offices, and he shall have Power to grant Reprieves and Pardons for Offences against the United States, except in Cases of Impeachment.

He shall have Power, by and with the Advice and Consent of the Senate, to make Treaties, provided two thirds of the Senators present concur; and he shall nominate, and by and with the Advice and Consent of the Senate, shall appoint Ambassadors, other public Ministers and Consuls, Judges of the supreme Court, and all other Officers of the United States, whose Appointments are not herein otherwise provided for, and which shall be established by Law: but the Congress may by Law vest the Appointment of such inferior Officers, as they think proper, in the President alone, in the Courts of Law, or in the Heads of Departments.

The President shall have Power to fill up all Vacancies that may happen during the Recess of the Senate, by granting Commissions which shall expire at the End of their next Session.

Section. 3.

He shall from time to time give to the Congress Information of the State of the Union, and recommend to their Consideration such Measures as he shall judge necessary and expedient; he may, on extraordinary Occasions, convene both Houses, or either of them, and in Case of Disagreement between them, with Respect to the Time of Adjournment, he may adjourn them to such Time as he shall think proper; he shall receive Ambassadors and other public Ministers; he shall take Care that the Laws be faithfully executed, and shall Commission all the Officers of the United States.

Section. 4.

The President, Vice President and all civil Officers of the United States, shall be removed from Office on Impeachment for, and Conviction of, Treason, Bribery, or other high Crimes and Misdemeanors.

Article. III.

Section. 1.

The judicial Power of the United States shall be vested in one supreme Court, and in such inferior Courts as the Congress may from time to time ordain and establish. The Judges, both of the supreme and inferior Courts, shall hold their Offices during good Behaviour, and shall, at stated Times, receive for their Services a Compensation, which shall not be diminished during their Continuance in Office.

Section. 2.

The judicial Power shall extend to all Cases, in Law and Equity, arising under this Constitution, the Laws of the United States, and Treaties made, or which shall be made, under their Authority;—to all Cases affecting Ambassadors, other public Ministers and Consuls;—to all Cases of admiralty and maritime Jurisdiction;—to Controversies to which the United States shall be a Party;—to Controversies between two or more States;—between a State and Citizens of another State;—between Citizens of different States;—between Citizens of the same State claiming Lands under Grants of different States, and between a State, or the Citizens thereof, and foreign States, Citizens or Subjects.

In all Cases affecting Ambassadors, other public Ministers and Consuls, and those in which a State shall be Party, the supreme Court shall have original Jurisdiction. In all the other Cases before mentioned, the supreme Court shall have appellate Jurisdiction, both as to Law and Fact, with such Exceptions, and under such Regulations as the Congress shall make.

The Trial of all Crimes, except in Cases of Impeachment, shall be by Jury; and such Trial shall be held in the State where the said Crimes shall have been committed; but when not committed within any State, the Trial shall be at such Place or Places as the Congress may by Law have directed.

Section. 3.

Treason against the United States, shall consist only in levying War against them, or in adhering to their Enemies, giving them Aid and Comfort. No Person shall be convicted of Treason unless on the Testimony of two Witnesses to the same overt Act, or on Confession in open Court.

The Congress shall have Power to declare the Punishment of Treason, but no Attainder of Treason shall work Corruption of Blood, or Forfeiture except during the Life of the Person attainted.

Article. IV.

Section. 1.

Full Faith and Credit shall be given in each State to the public Acts, Records, and judicial Proceedings of every other State. And the Congress may by general Laws prescribe the Manner in which such Acts, Records and Proceedings shall be proved, and the Effect thereof.

Section. 2.

The Citizens of each State shall be entitled to all Privileges and Immunities of Citizens in the several States.

A Person charged in any State with Treason, Felony, or other Crime, who shall flee from Justice, and be found in another State, shall on Demand of the executive Authority of the State from which he fled, be delivered up, to be removed to the State having Jurisdiction of the Crime.

No Person held to Service or Labour in one State, under the Laws thereof, escaping into another, shall, in Consequence of any Law or Regulation therein, be discharged from such Service or Labour, but shall be delivered up on Claim of the Party to whom such Service or Labour may be due.

Section. 3.

New States may be admitted by the Congress into this Union; but no new State shall be formed or erected within the Jurisdiction of any other State; nor any State be formed by the Junction of two or more States, or Parts of States, without the Consent of the Legislatures of the States concerned as well as of the Congress.

The Congress shall have Power to dispose of and make all needful Rules and Regulations respecting the Territory or other Property belonging to the United States; and nothing in this Constitution shall be so construed as to Prejudice any Claims of the United States, or of any particular State.

Section. 4.

The United States shall guarantee to every State in this Union a Republican Form of Government, and shall protect each of them against Invasion; and on Application of the Legislature, or of the Executive (when the Legislature cannot be convened), against domestic Violence.

Article. V.

The Congress, whenever two thirds of both Houses shall deem it necessary, shall propose Amendments to this Constitution, or, on the Application of the Legislatures of two thirds of the several States, shall call a Convention for proposing Amendments, which, in either Case, shall be valid to all Intents and Purposes, as Part of this Constitution, when ratified by the Legislatures of three fourths of the several States, or by Conventions in three fourths thereof, as the one or the other Mode of Ratification may be proposed by the Congress; Provided that no Amendment which may be made prior to the Year One thousand eight hundred and eight shall in any Manner affect the first and fourth Clauses in the Ninth Section of the first Article; and that no State, without its Consent, shall be deprived of its equal Suffrage in the Senate.

Article. VI.

All Debts contracted and Engagements entered into, before the Adoption of this Constitution, shall be as valid against the United States under this Constitution, as under the Confederation.

This Constitution, and the Laws of the United States which shall be made in Pursuance thereof; and all Treaties made, or which shall be made, under the Authority of the United States, shall be the supreme Law of the Land; and the Judges in every State shall be bound thereby, any Thing in the Constitution or Laws of any State to the Contrary notwithstanding.

The Senators and Representatives before mentioned, and the Members of the several State Legislatures, and all executive and judicial Officers, both of the United States and of the several States, shall be bound by Oath or Affirmation, to support this Constitution; but no religious Test shall ever be required as a Qualification to any Office or public Trust under the United States.

Article. VII.

The Ratification of the Conventions of nine States, shall be sufficient for the Establishment of this Constitution between the States so
ratifying the Same.

*The Word, "the," being interlined between the seventh and eighth Lines of
the first Page, the Word "Thirty" being partly written on an Erazure in the fif-
teenth Line of the first Page, The Words "is tried" being interlined between the
thirty second and thirty third Lines of the first Page and the Word "the" being
interlined between the forty third and forty fourth Lines of the second Page.*
Attest William Jackson Secretary

Done in Convention by the Unanimous Consent of the States present the Seventeenth Day of September in the Year of our Lord one
thousand seven hundred and Eighty seven and of the Independence
of the United States of America the Twelfth[.] In witness whereof
We have hereunto subscribed our Names,

G°. Washington Presidt *and deputy from Virginia*

Delaware Geo: Read Gunning Bedford jun John
Dickinson Richard Bassett Jaco: Broom
Maryland James McHenry Dan of St Thos.
Jenifer Danl. Carroll
Virginia John Blair James Madison Jr.
North Carolina Wm. Blount Richd. Dobbs
Spaight Hu Williamson
South Carolina J. Rutledge Charles Cotesworth
Pinckney Charles Pinckney Pierce Butler
Georgia William Few Abr Baldwin
New Hampshire John Langdon Nicholas Gilman
Massachusetts Nathaniel Gorham Rufus King
Connecticut Wm. Saml. Johnson Roger Sherman
New York Alexander Hamilton
New Jersey Wil: Livingston David Brearley Wm.
Paterson Jona: Dayton
Pennsylvania B Franklin Thomas Mifflin Robt.
Morris Geo. Clymer Thos. FitzSimons Jared
Ingersoll James Wilson Gouv Morris

NOTES: OBJECTIONS TO THE CONSTITUTION BY GEORGE MASON OF VIRGINIA

("This government will set out a moderate aristocracy: it is at present impossible to foresee whether it will, in its operation, produce a monarchy, or a corrupt tyrannical aristocracy")

OCTOBER 1787

Virginia's George Mason (1725–1792), one of the most important and active delegates at the Convention, refused to sign the Constitution. As the author of Virginia's Declaration of Rights he had many fears about the absence of a bill of rights in this constitution, and though he continued to oppose its ratification in Virginia, his objections helped prepare the way for the Bill of Rights in 1791. Mason wrote these notes on a rough draft of the Constitution.

There is no Declaration of Rights, and the laws of the general government being paramount to the laws and constitutions of the several states, the Declarations of Rights in the separate states are no security. Nor are the people secured even in the enjoyment of the benefits of the common law.

In the House of Representatives, there is not the substance, but the shadow only of representation; which can never produce proper information in the legislature, or inspire confidence in the people; the laws will therefore be generally made by men little concerned in, and unacquainted with their effects and consequences.

The Senate have the power of altering all money bills, and of originating appropriations of money, and the salaries of the officers of their own appointment, in conjunction with the president of the United States; although they are not the representatives of the people, or amenable to them.

These, with their other great powers (viz: their power in the appointment of ambassadors and all public officers, in making treaties, and in trying all impeachments), their influence upon and connection with the supreme executive from these causes, their duration of office, and their being a constant existing body, almost continually sitting, joined with their being one complete branch of the legislature will destroy any balance in the government, and enable them to accomplish what usurpations they please upon the rights and liberty of the people.

The judiciary of the United States is so constructed and extended, as to absorb and destroy the judiciaries of the several states; thereby rendering law as tedious, intricate and expensive, and justice as unattainable, by a great part of the community, as in England, and enabling the rich to oppress and ruin the poor.

The President of the United States has no constitutional council (a thing unknown in any safe and regular government); he will therefore be unsupported by proper information and advice; and will generally be directed by minions and favorites. Or he will become a tool to the Senate — or a council of state will grow out of the principal officers of the great departments; the worst and most dangerous of all ingredients for such a council, in a free country.

From this fatal defect has arisen the improper power of the Senate in the appointment of public officers, and the alarming dependence and connection between that branch of the legislature and the supreme executive.

Hence also sprung that unnecessary officer, the Vice-President; who for want of other employment is made President of the Senate; thereby dangerously blending the executive and legislative powers; besides always giving to some one of the states an unnecessary and unjust preeminence over the others.

The President of the United States has the unrestrained power of granting pardons for treason; which may be sometimes exercised to screen from punishment those whom he had secretly instigated to commit the crime, and thereby prevent a discovery of his own guilt.

By declaring all treaties supreme laws of the land, the executive and the Senate have in many cases an exclusive power of legislation; which might have been avoided by proper distinctions with respect to treaties, and requiring the assent of the House of Representatives, where it could be done, with safety.

By requiring a majority to make all commercial and navigation laws, the five Southern states (whose produce and circumstances are totally different from that of the eight Northern and Eastern states) may be ruined; for such rigid and premature regulations may be made, as will enable the merchants of the Northern and Eastern states not only to demand an exorbitant freight, but to monopolize the purchase of the commodities at their own price, for many years; to the great Injury of the landed interest, and impoverishment of the people; and the danger is the greater, as the gain on one side will be in proportion to the loss on the other. Whereas requiring two thirds of the members present in both Houses would have produced mutual moderation, promoted the general interest, and removed an insuperable objection to the adoption of this government.

Under their own construction of the general clause, at the end of the enumerated powers, the Congress may grant monopolies in trade and commerce, constitute new crimes, inflict unusual and severe punishments, and extend their powers as far as they shall think proper; so that the state legislatures have no security for their powers now presumed to remain to them, or the people for their rights.

There is no declaration of any kind, for preserving the liberty of the press, or the trial by jury in civil causes; nor against the danger of standing armies in time of peace.

The state legislatures are restrained from laying import duties on their own produce.

Both the general legislature★ and the state legislatures are expressly prohibited making ex post facto laws: though there never was, nor can be a legislature but must and will make such laws, when necessity and the public safety require them; which will hereafter be a breach of all the Constitutions in the Union, and afford precedents for other innovations.

This government will set out a moderate aristocracy: it is at present impossible to foresee whether it will, in its operation, produce a monarchy, or a corrupt tyrannical aristocracy; it will most probably vibrate some years between the two, and then terminate in the one or the other.

[★ *Mason's note*: The general Legislature is restrained from prohibiting the further Importation of Slaves for twenty odd years; tho' such Importations render the United States weaker, more vulnerable, and less capable of Defence.]

ARTICLE, *CENTINEL* NO. 1, "TO THE FREEMEN OF PENNSYLVANIA," BY SAMUEL BRYAN

("The constitution of Pennsylvania is yet in existence, as yet you have the right to freedom of speech and of publishing your sentiments")

PHILADELPHIA, *INDEPENDENT GAZETTEER*
OCTOBER 5, 1787

Samuel Bryan (1759–1821) of Philadelphia was one of many Americans who saw more freedom and protection under his own state constitution than under the new proposed federal constitution. He wrote approximately two dozen essays in this Centinel series.

Friends, Countrymen and Fellow Citizens,

Permit one of yourselves to put you in mind of certain liberties and privileges secured to you by the constitution of this commonwealth, and to beg your serious attention to his uninterested opinion upon the plan of federal government submitted to your consideration, before you surrender these great and valuable privileges up forever.

Your present frame of government secures to you a right to hold yourselves, houses, papers and possessions free from search and seizure, and therefore warrants granted without oaths or affirmations first made, affording sufficient foundation for them, whereby any officer or messenger may be commanded or required to search your houses or seize your persons or property, not particularly described in such warrant, shall not be granted. Your constitution further provides "that in controversies respecting property, and in suits between man and man, the parties have a right to trial by jury, which ought to be held sacred." It also provides and declares: "that the people have a right of FREEDOM OF SPEECH, and of WRITING and PUBLISHING their sentiments, therefore THE FREEDOM OF THE PRESS OUGHT NOT TO BE RESTRAINED." The constitution of Pennsylvania is yet in existence, as yet you have the right to freedom of speech and of

86

publishing your sentiments. How long those rights will appertain to you, you yourselves are called upon to say, whether your houses shall continue to be your castles; whether your papers, your persons and your property, are to be held sacred and free from general warrants, you are now to determine. Whether the trial by jury is to continue as your birthright, the freemen of Pennsylvania, nay, of all America, are now called upon to declare.

Without presuming upon my own judgment, I cannot think it an unwarrantable presumption to offer my private opinion, and call upon others for theirs; and if I use my pen with the boldness of a free man, it is because I know that the liberty of the press yet remains un-violated, and juries yet are judges.

The late Convention have submitted to your consideration a plan of a new federal government. The subject is highly interesting to your future welfare. Whether it be calculated to promote the great ends of civil society, viz. the happiness and prosperity of the community; it behooves you well to consider, uninfluenced by the authority of names. Instead of that frenzy of enthusiasm that has actuated the citizens of Philadelphia, in their approbation of the proposed plan, before it was possible that it could be the result of a rational investigation into its principles; it ought to be dispassionately and deliberately examined, and its own intrinsic merit the only criterion of your patronage. If ever free and unbiased discussion was proper or necessary, it is on such an occasion. All the blessings of liberty and the dearest privileges of free-men are now at stake and dependent on your present conduct. Those who are competent to the task of developing the principles of gov-ernment, ought to be encouraged to come forward, and thereby the better enable the people to make a proper judgment; for the science of government is so abstruse, that few are able to judge for themselves: without such assistance the people are too apt to yield an implicit as-sent to the opinions of those characters, whose abilities are held in the highest esteem, and to those in whose integrity and patriotism they can confide: not considering that the love of domination is generally in proportion to talents, abilities, and superior acquirements; and that the men of the greatest purity of intention may be made instruments of despotism in the hands of the artful and designing. If it were not for the stability and attachment which time and habit gives to forms of government, it would be in the power of the enlightened and as-piring few, if they should combine, at any time to destroy the best establishments, and even make the people the instruments of their own subjugation.

The late revolution having effaced in a great measure all former habits, and the present institutions are so recent, that there exists not that great reluctance to innovation, so remarkable in old communities, and which accords with reason, for the most comprehensive mind cannot foresee the full operation of material changes on civil polity; it is the genius of the common law to resist innovation.

The wealthy and ambitious, who in every community think they have a right to lord it over their fellow creatures, have availed themselves, very successfully, of this favorable disposition; for the people thus unsettled in their sentiments, have been prepared to accede to any extreme of government; all the distresses and difficulties they experience, proceeding from various causes, have been ascribed to the impotency of the present confederation, and thence they have been led to expect full relief from the adoption of the proposed system of government; and in the other event, immediately ruin and annihilation as a nation. These characters flatter themselves that they have lulled all distrust and jealousy of their new plan, by gaining the concurrence of the two men in whom America has the highest confidence,[4] and now triumphantly exult in the completion of their long meditated schemes of power and aggrandizement. I would be very far from insinuating that the two illustrious personages alluded to, have not the welfare of their country at heart; but that the unsuspecting goodness and zeal of the one, has been imposed on, in a subject of which he must be necessarily inexperienced, from his other arduous engagements; and that the weakness and indecision attendant on old age, has been practiced on in the other.

I am fearful that the principles of government inculcated in Mr. Adams's treatise, and enforced in the numerous essays and paragraphs in the newspapers, have misled some well designing members of the late Convention. But it will appear in the sequel, that the construction of the proposed plan of government is infinitely more extravagant.

I have been anxiously expecting that some enlightened patriot would, ere this, have taken up the pen to expose the futility, and counteract the baneful tendency of such principles. Mr. Adams's sine qua non of a good government is three balancing powers, whose repelling qualities are to produce an equilibrium of interests, and thereby promote the happiness of the whole community. He asserts that the administrators of every government, will ever be actuated by views of private interest and ambition, to the prejudice of the public good; that therefore the only effectual method to secure the rights of the people and promote their welfare, is to create an opposition of interests between the members of two distinct bodies, in the exercise of the powers of government, and balanced by those of a third. This hypothesis

---

[4] Bryan means George Washington and Benjamin Franklin.

supposes human wisdom competent to the task of instituting three co-equal orders in government, and a corresponding weight in the community to enable them respectively to exercise their several parts, and whose views and interests should be so distinct as to prevent a co-alition of any two of them for the destruction of the third. Mr. Adams, although he has traced the constitution of every form of government that ever existed, as far as history affords materials, has not been able to adduce a single instance of such a government; he indeed says that the British constitution is such in theory, but this is rather a confirmation that his principles are chimerical and not to be reduced to practice. If such an organization of power were practicable, how long would it continue? Not a day—for there is so great a disparity in the talents, wisdom and industry of mankind, that the scale would presently preponderate to one or the other body, and with every accession of power the means of further increase would be greatly extended. The state of society in England is much more favorable to such a scheme of government than that of America. There they have a powerful hereditary nobility, and real distinctions of rank and interests; but even there, for want of that perfect equality of power and distinction of interests, in the three orders of government, they exist but in name; the only operative and efficient check, upon the conduct of administration, is the sense of the people at large.

Suppose a government could be formed and supported on such principles, would it answer the great purposes of civil society; if the administrators of every government are actuated by views of private interest and ambition, how is the welfare and happiness of the community to be the result of such jarring adverse interests?

Therefore, as different orders in government will not produce the good of the whole, we must recur to other principles. I believe it will be found that the form of government, which holds those entrusted with power, in the greatest responsibility to their constituents, the best calculated for freemen. A republican, or free government, can only exist where the body of the people are virtuous, and where property is pretty equally divided; in such a government the people are the sovereign and their sense or opinion is the criterion of every public measure; for when this ceases to be the case, the nature of the government is changed, and an aristocracy, monarchy or despotism will rise on its ruin. The highest responsibility is to be attained, in a simple structure of government, for the great body of the people never steadily attend to the operations of government, and for want of due information are liable to be imposed on. If you complicate the plan by various orders, the people will be perplexed and divided in their sentiments about the source of abuses or misconduct, some will impute it to the senate, others to the house of representatives, and so on, that the interposition of the people may be rendered imperfect or perhaps wholly abortive. But if, imitating the constitution of Pennsylvania, you vest all the legislative power in one body of men (separating the executive and judicial) elected for a short period, and necessarily excluded by rotation from permanency, and guarded from precipitancy and surprise by delays imposed on its proceedings, you will create the most perfect responsibility, for then, whenever the people feel a grievance they cannot mistake the authors, and will apply the remedy with certainty and effect, discarding them at the next election. This tie of responsibility will obviate all the dangers apprehended from a single legislature, and will the best secure the rights of the people.

Having premised this much, I shall now proceed to the examination of the proposed plan of government, and I trust, shall make it appear to the meanest capacity, that it has none of the essential requisites of a free government; that it is neither founded on those balancing restraining powers, recommended by Mr. Adams and attempted in the British constitution, or possessed of that responsibility to its constituents, which, in my opinion, is the only effectual security for the liberties and happiness of the people; but on the contrary, that it is a most daring attempt to establish a despotic aristocracy among freemen, that the world has ever witnessed.

I shall previously consider the extent of the powers intended to be vested in Congress, before I examine the construction of the general government.

It will not be controverted that the legislative is the highest delegated power in government, and that all others are subordinate to it. The celebrated Montesquieu establishes it as a maxim, that legislation necessarily follow the power of taxation. By Section 8, of the first article of the proposed plan of government, "the Congress are to have power to lay and collect taxes, duties, imposts and excises, to pay the debts and provide for the common defence and general welfare of the United States; but all duties, imposts and excises, shall be uniform throughout the United States."

Now what can be more comprehensive than these words? Not content by other sections of this plan, to grant all the great executive powers of a confederation, and a STANDING ARMY IN TIME OF PEACE, that grand engine of oppression, and moreover the absolute control over the commerce of the United States and all external objects of revenue, such as unlimited imposts upon imports, etc.—they are to be vested with every species of internal taxation;—whatever taxes, duties and excises that they may deem requisite for the general welfare, may be imposed on the citizens of these states, levied by the offices of Congress, distributed through every district in America; and the collection would be enforced by the standing army, however grievous or improper they may be. The Congress may construe every purpose for which the state legislatures now lay taxes, to be for the general welfare, and thereby seize upon every object of revenue.

The judicial power by first sect. of Article 3 "shall extend to all cases, in law and equity, arising under this constitution, the laws of the United States, and treaties made or which shall be made under their authority; to all cases affecting ambassadors, other public ministers and consuls; to all cases of admiralty and maritime jurisdiction, to controversies to which the United States shall be a party, to controversies between two or more states, between a state and citizens of another state, between citizens of different states, between citizens of the same state claiming lands under grants of different states, and between a state, or the citizens thereof, and foreign states, citizens or subjects."

. The judicial power to be vested in one Supreme Court, and in such Inferior Courts as the Congress may from time to time ordain and establish.

The objects of jurisdiction recited above are so numerous, and the shades of distinction between civil causes are oftentimes so slight, that it is more than probable that the state judicatories would be wholly superseded; for in contests about jurisdiction, the federal court, as the most powerful, would ever prevail. Every person acquainted with the history of the courts in England knows by what ingenious sophisms they have, at different periods, extended the sphere of their jurisdiction over objects out of the line of their institution, and contrary to their very nature; courts of a criminal jurisdiction obtaining cognizance in civil causes.

To put the omnipotency of Congress over the state government and judicatories out of all doubt, the sixth article ordains that "this constitution and the laws of the United States which shall be made in pursuance thereof, and all treaties made, or which shall be made under the authority of the United States, shall be the supreme law of the land, and the judges in every state shall be bound thereby, anything in the constitution or laws of any state to the contrary notwithstanding."

By these sections the all-prevailing power of taxation, and such extensive legislative and judicial powers are vested in the general government, as must in their operation, necessarily absorb the state legislature and judicatories; and that such was in the contemplation of the framers of it, will appear from the provision made for such event, in another part of it (but that, fearful of alarming the people by so great an innovation, they have suffered the forms of the separate governments to remain, as a blind). By section 4 of the first article, "the times, places and manner of holding elections for senators and representatives, shall be prescribed in each state by the legislature thereof; but the Congress may at any time, by law, make or alter such regulations, except to the place of chusing senators." The plain construction of which is, that when the state legislatures drop out of sight, from the necessary operation of this government, then Congress are to provide for the election and appointment of representatives and senators.

If the foregoing be a just comment — if the United States are to be melted down into one empire, it becomes you to consider, whether such a government, however constructed, would be eligible in so extended a territory; and whether it would be practicable, consistent with freedom? It is the opinion of the greatest writers that a very extensive country cannot be governed on democratical principles, on any other plan, than a confederation of a number of small republics, possessing all the powers of internal government, but united in the management of their foreign and general concerns.

It would not be difficult to prove that any thing short of despotism could not bind so great a country under one government; and that whatever plan you might, at the first setting out, establish, it would issue in a despotism.

If one general government could be instituted and maintained on principles of freedom, it would not be so competent to attend to the various local concerns and wants, of every particular district, as well as the peculiar governments, who are nearer the scene, and possessed of superior means of information; besides, if the business of the whole union is to be managed by one government, there would not be time. Do we not already see, that the inhabitants in a number of larger states, who are remote from the seat of government, are loudly complaining of the inconveniences and disadvantages they are subjected to on this account, and that, to enjoy the comforts of local government, they are separating into smaller divisions.

Having taken a review of the powers, I shall now examine the construction of the proposed general government.

Article I. Section 1. "All legislative powers herein granted shall be vested in a Congress of the United States, which shall consist of a senate and house of representatives." By another section, the president (the principal executive officer) has a conditional control over their proceedings.

Section 2. "The house of representatives shall be composed of members chosen every second year, by the people of the several states.

The number of representatives shall not exceed one for every 30,000 inhabitants."

The senate, the other constituent branch of the legislature, is formed by the legislature of each state appointing two senators, for the term of six years.

The executive power by Article 2, Section 1 is to be vested in a president of the United States of America, elected for four years: Section 2 gives him "power, by and with the consent of the senate to make treaties, provided two thirds of the senators present concur; and he shall nominate, and by and with the advice and consent of the senate, shall appoint ambassadors, other public ministers and consuls, judges of the Supreme Court, and all other officers of the United States, whose appointments are not herein otherwise provided for, and which shall be established by law, etc." And by another section he has the absolute power of granting reprieves and pardons for treason and all other high crimes and misdemeanors, except in case of impeachment.

The foregoing are the outlines of the plan. Thus we see, the house of representatives are on the part of the people to balance the senate, who I suppose will be composed of the better sort, the well born, etc. The number of the representatives (being only one for every 30,000 inhabitants) appears to be too few, either to communicate the requisite information, of the wants, local circumstances and sentiments of so extensive an empire, or to present corruption and undue influence, in the exercise of such great powers; the term for which they are to be chosen, too long to preserve a due dependence and accountability to their constituents; and the mode and places of their election not sufficiently ascertained, for as Congress have the control over both, they may govern the choice by ordering the representatives of a whole state, to be elected in one place, and that too may be the most inconvenient.

The senate, the great efficient body in this plan of government, is constituted on the most unequal principles. The smallest state in the union has equal weight with the great states of Virginia, Massachusetts, or Pennsylvania. The Senate, besides its legislative functions, has a very considerable share in the Executive; none of the principal appointments to office can be made without its advice and consent. The term and mode of its appointment will lead to permanency; the members are chosen for six years, the mode is under the control of Congress, and as there is no exclusion by rotation, they may be continued for life, which, from their extensive means of influence, would follow of course. The President, who would be a mere pageant of state, unless he coincides with the views of the Senate, would either become the head of the aristocratic junto in that body, or its minion; besides, their influence being the most predominant, could the best secure his re-election to office. And from his power of granting pardons, he might screen from punishment the most treasonable attempts on the liberties of the people, when instigated by the Senate.

From this investigation into the organization of this government, it appears that it is devoid of all responsibility or accountability to the great body of the people, and that so far from being a regular balanced government, it would be in practice a permanent ARISTOCRACY.

The framers of it, actuated by the true spirit of such a government, which ever abominates and suppresses all free enquiry and discussion, have made no provision for the liberty of the press, that grant palladium of freedom, and scourge of tyrants; but observed a total silence on that head. It is the opinion of some great writers, that if the liberty of the press, by an institution of religion, or otherwise, could be rendered sacred, even in Turkey, that despotism would fly before it. And it is worthy of remark, that there is no declaration of personal rights, premised in most free constitutions; and that trial by jury in civil cases is taken away; for what other construction can be put on the following, viz. Article III. Section 2: "In all cases affecting ambassadors, other public ministers and consuls, and those in which a State shall be party, the Supreme Court shall have original jurisdiction. In all the other cases above mentioned, the Supreme Court shall have appellate jurisdiction, both as to law and fact"? It would be a novelty in jurisprudence, as well as evidently improper to allow an appeal from the verdict of a jury, on the matter of fact; therefore, it implies and allows of a dismission of the jury in civil cases, and especially when it is considered, that jury trial in criminal cases is expressly stipulated for, but not in civil cases.

But our situation is represented to be so critically dreadful, that, however reprehensible and exceptionable the proposed plan of government may be, there is no alternative, between the adoption of it and absolute ruin.—My fellow citizens, things are not at that crisis, it is the argument of tyrants; the present distracted state of Europe secures us from injury on that quarter, and as to domestic dissentions, we have not so much to fear from them, as to precipitate us into this form of government, without it is a safe and a proper one. For remember, of all possible evils, that of despotism is the worst and the most to be dreaded.

Besides, it cannot be supposed, that the first essay on so difficult a subject, is so well digested, as it ought to be,—if the proposed plan, after a mature deliberation, should meet the approbation of the respective states, the matter will end; but if it should be found to be fraught with dangers and inconveniences, a future general Convention being in possession of the objections, will be the better enabled to plan a suitable government.

> *Who's here so base, that would be a bondman be?*
> *If any, speak; for him have I offended.*
> *Who's here so vile, that will not love his country?*
> *If any, speak, for him have I offended.*[5]

---

[5] Bryan is paraphrasing Brutus's speech from Act III, Scene 2, in Shakespeare's *Julius Caesar.*

ARTICLE, *THE FEDERALIST*, NO. 10: "THE UNION AS A SAFEGUARD AGAINST DOMESTIC FACTION AND INSURRECTION," BY JAMES MADISON

("... the *causes* of faction cannot be removed, and ... relief is only to be sought in the means of controlling its *effects*")

NOVEMBER 22, 1787

The eighty-five essays that make up the Federalist Papers were composed by John Jay, Alexander Hamilton, and James Madison to convince the voters of New York to ratify the Constitution. Though written for newspapers at the rate of two or three a week from the fall of 1787 into the late spring of 1788, their haste did not deter their power in fending off anti-Federalist attacks and illuminating every major point of the Constitution. Thomas Jefferson declared the collection "the best commentary on the principles of government which was ever written." This essay embodies some of Madison's boldest, most important ideas. (The originally untitled articles were all signed "Publius," as the team of authors sought to persuade voters without calling attention to each man's own, well-known, occasionally contradictory personal views.)

To the People of the State of New York:

Among the numerous advantages promised by a well-constructed Union, none deserves to be more accurately developed than its tendency to break and control the violence of faction. The friend of popular governments never finds himself so much alarmed for their character and fate, as when he contemplates their propensity to this dangerous vice. He will not fail, therefore, to set a due value on any plan which, without violating the principles to which he is attached, provides a proper cure for it. The instability, injustice, and confusion introduced into the public councils, have, in truth, been the mortal diseases under which popular governments have everywhere perished;

as they continue to be the favorite and fruitful topics from which the adversaries to liberty derive their most specious declamations. The valuable improvements made by the American constitutions on the popular models, both ancient and modern, cannot certainly be too much admired; but it would be an unwarrantable partiality, to contend that they have as effectually obviated the danger on this side, as was wished and expected. Complaints are everywhere heard from our most considerate and virtuous citizens, equally the friends of public and private faith, and of public and personal liberty, that our governments are too unstable, that the public good is disregarded in the conflicts of rival parties, and that measures are too often decided, not according to the rules of justice and the rights of the minor party, but by the superior force of an interested and overbearing majority. However anxiously we may wish that these complaints had no foundation, the evidence, of known facts will not permit us to deny that they are in some degree true. It will be found, indeed, on a candid review of our situation, that some of the distresses under which we labor have been erroneously charged on the operation of our governments; but it will be found, at the same time, that other causes will not alone account for many of our heaviest misfortunes; and, particularly, for that prevailing and increasing distrust of public engagements, and alarm for private rights, which are echoed from one end of the continent to the other. These must be chiefly, if not wholly, effects of the unsteadiness and injustice with which a factious spirit has tainted our public administrations.

By a faction, I understand a number of citizens, whether amounting to a majority or a minority of the whole, who are united and actuated by some common impulse of passion, or of interest, adversed to the rights of other citizens, or to the permanent and aggregate interests of the community.

There are two methods of curing the mischiefs of faction: the one, by removing its causes; the other, by controlling its effects.

There are again two methods of removing the causes of faction: the one, by destroying the liberty which is essential to its existence; the other, by giving to every citizen the same opinions, the same passions, and the same interests.

It could never be more truly said than of the first remedy, that it was worse than the disease. Liberty is to faction what air is to fire, an aliment without which it instantly expires. But it could not be less folly to abolish liberty, which is essential to political life, because it nourishes faction, than it would be to wish the annihilation of air, which is essential to animal life, because it imparts to fire its destructive agency.

The second expedient is as impracticable as the first would be unwise. As long as the reason of man continues fallible, and he is at liberty to exercise it, different opinions will be formed. As long as the connection subsists between his reason and his self-love, his opinions and his passions will have a reciprocal influence on each other; and the former will be objects to which the latter will attach themselves. The diversity in the faculties of men, from which the rights of property originate, is not less an insuperable obstacle to a uniformity of interests. The protection of these faculties is the first object of government. From the protection of different and unequal faculties of acquiring property, the possession of different degrees and kinds of property immediately results; and from the influence of these on the sentiments and views of the respective proprietors, ensues a division of the society into different interests and parties.

The latent causes of faction are thus sown in the nature of man; and we see them everywhere brought into different degrees of activity, according to the different circumstances of civil society. A zeal for different opinions concerning religion, concerning government, and many other points, as well of speculation as of practice; an attachment to different leaders ambitiously contending for pre-eminence and power; or to persons of other descriptions whose fortunes have been interesting to the human passions, have, in turn, divided mankind into parties, inflamed them with mutual animosity, and rendered them much more disposed to vex and oppress each other than to co-operate for their common good. So strong is this propensity of mankind to fall into mutual animosities, that where no substantial occasion presents itself, the most frivolous and fanciful distinctions have been sufficient to kindle their unfriendly passions and excite their most violent conflicts. But the most common and durable source of factions has been the various and unequal distribution of property. Those who hold and those who are without property have ever formed distinct interests in society. Those who are creditors, and those who are debtors, fall under a like discrimination. A landed interest, a manufacturing interest, a mercantile interest, a moneyed interest, with many lesser interests, grow up of necessity in civilized nations, and divide them into different classes, actuated by different sentiments and views. The regulation of these various and interfering interests forms the principal task of modern legislation, and involves the spirit of party and faction in the necessary and ordinary operations of the government.

No man is allowed to be a judge in his own cause, because his interest would certainly bias his judgment, and, not improbably, corrupt his integrity. With equal, nay with greater reason, a body of men are unfit to be both judges and parties at the same time; yet what are many of the most important acts of legislation, but so many judicial determinations, not indeed concerning the rights of single persons, but concerning the rights of large bodies of citizens? And what are the different classes of legislators but advocates and parties to the causes which they determine? Is a law proposed concerning private debts? It is a question to which the creditors are parties on one side and the debtors on the other. Justice ought to hold the balance between them. Yet the parties are, and must be, themselves the judges; and the most numerous party, or, in other words, the most powerful faction must be expected to prevail. Shall domestic manufactures be encouraged, and in what degree, by restrictions on foreign manufactures? are questions which would be differently decided by the landed and the manufacturing classes, and probably by neither with a sole regard to justice and the public good. The apportionment of taxes on the various descriptions of property is an act which seems to require the most exact impartiality; yet there is, perhaps, no legislative act in which greater opportunity and temptation are given to a predominant party to trample on the rules of justice. Every shilling with which they overburden the inferior number is a shilling saved to their own pockets.

It is in vain to say that enlightened statesmen will be able to adjust these clashing interests, and render them all subservient to the public good. Enlightened statesmen will not always be at the helm. Nor, in many cases, can such an adjustment be made at all without taking into view indirect and remote considerations, which will rarely prevail over the immediate interest which one party may find in disregarding the rights of another or the good of the whole.

The inference to which we are brought is, that the CAUSES of faction cannot be removed, and that relief is only to be sought in the means of controlling its EFFECTS.

If a faction consists of less than a majority, relief is supplied by the republican principle, which enables the majority to defeat its sinister views by regular vote. It may clog the administration, it may convulse the society; but it will be unable to execute and mask its violence under the forms of the Constitution. When a majority is included in a faction, the form of popular government, on the other hand, enables it to sacrifice to its ruling passion or interest both the public good and the rights of other citizens. To secure the public good and private rights against the danger of such a faction, and at the same time to preserve the spirit and the form of popular government, is then the great object to which our inquiries are directed. Let me add that it is the great desideratum by which this form of government can be rescued from the opprobrium under which it has so long labored, and be recommended to the esteem and adoption of mankind.

By what means is this object attainable? Evidently by one of two only. Either the existence of the same passion or interest in a majority at the same time must be prevented, or the majority, having such coexistent passion or interest, must be rendered, by their number and local situation, unable to concert and carry into effect schemes of oppression. If the impulse and the opportunity be suffered to coincide, we well know that neither moral nor religious motives can be relied on as an adequate control. They are not found to be such on the injustice and violence of individuals, and lose their efficacy in proportion to the number combined together, that is, in proportion as their efficacy becomes needful.

From this view of the subject it may be concluded that a pure democracy, by which I mean a society consisting of a small number of citizens, who assemble and administer the government in person, can admit of no cure for the mischiefs of faction. A common passion or interest will, in almost every case, be felt by a majority of the whole; a communication and concert result from the form of government itself; and there is nothing to check the inducements to sacrifice the weaker party or an obnoxious individual. Hence it is that such democracies have ever been spectacles of turbulence and contention; have ever been found incompatible with personal security or the rights of property; and have in general been as short in their lives as they have been violent in their deaths. Theoretic politicians, who have patronized this species of government, have erroneously supposed that by reducing mankind to a perfect equality in their political rights, they would, at the same time, be perfectly equalized and assimilated in their possessions, their opinions, and their passions.

A republic, by which I mean a government in which the scheme of representation takes place, opens a different prospect, and promises the cure for which we are seeking. Let us examine the points in which it varies from pure democracy, and we shall comprehend both the nature of the cure and the efficacy which it must derive from the Union.

The two great points of difference between a democracy and a republic are: first, the delegation of the government, in the latter, to a small number of citizens elected by the rest; secondly, the greater number of citizens, and greater sphere of country, over which the latter may be extended.

The effect of the first difference is, on the one hand, to refine and enlarge the public views, by passing them through the medium of a chosen body of citizens, whose wisdom may best discern the true interest of their country, and whose patriotism and love of justice will be least likely to sacrifice it to temporary or partial considerations. Under such a regulation, it may well happen that the public voice, pronounced by the representatives of the people, will be more consonant to the public good than if pronounced by the people themselves, convened for the purpose. On the other hand, the effect may be inverted. Men of factious tempers, of local prejudices, or of sinister designs, may, by intrigue, by corruption, or by other means, first obtain the suffrages, and then betray the interests, of the people. The question resulting is, whether small or extensive republics are more favorable to the election of proper guardians of the public weal; and it is clearly decided in favor of the latter by two obvious considerations:

In the first place, it is to be remarked that, however small the republic may be, the representatives must be raised to a certain number, in order to guard against the cabals of a few; and that, however large it may be, they must be limited to a certain number, in order to guard against the confusion of a multitude. Hence, the number of representatives in the two cases not being in proportion to that of the two constituents, and being proportionally greater in the small republic, it follows that, if the proportion of fit characters be not less in the large than in the small republic, the former will present a greater option, and consequently a greater probability of a fit choice.

In the next place, as each representative will be chosen by a greater number of citizens in the large than in the small republic, it will be more difficult for unworthy candidates to practice with success the vicious arts by which elections are too often carried; and the suffrages of the people being more free, will be more likely to centre in men who possess the most attractive merit and the most diffusive and established characters. It must be confessed that in this, as in most other cases, there is a mean, on both sides of which inconveniences will be found to lie. By enlarging too much the number of electors, you render the representatives too little acquainted with all their local circumstances and lesser interests; as by reducing it too much, you render him unduly attached to these, and too little fit to comprehend and pursue great and national objects. The federal Constitution forms a happy combination in this respect; the great and aggregate interests being referred to the national, the local and particular to the state legislatures.

The other point of difference is, the greater number of citizens and extent of territory which may be brought within the compass of republican than of democratic government; and it is this circumstance principally which renders factious combinations less to be dreaded in the former than in the latter. The smaller the society, the fewer probably will be the distinct parties and interests composing it; the fewer the distinct parties and interests, the more frequently will a majority be found of the same party; and the smaller the number of individuals composing a majority, and the smaller the compass within which they are placed, the more easily will they concert and execute their plans of oppression. Extend the sphere, and you take in a greater variety of parties and interests; you make it less probable that a majority of the whole will have a common motive to invade the rights of other citizens; or if such a common motive exists, it will be more difficult for all who feel it to discover their own strength, and to act in unison with each other. Besides other impediments, it may be remarked that, where there is a consciousness of unjust or dishonorable purposes, communication is always checked by distrust in proportion to the number whose concurrence is necessary.

Hence, it clearly appears, that the same advantage which a republic has over a democracy, in controlling the effects of faction, is enjoyed by a large over a small republic,—is enjoyed by the Union over the states composing it. Does the advantage consist in the substitution of representatives whose enlightened views and virtuous sentiments render them superior to local prejudices and schemes of injustice? It will not be denied that the representation of the Union will be most likely to possess these requisite endowments. Does it consist in the greater security afforded by a greater variety of parties, against the event of any one party being able to outnumber and oppress the rest? In an equal degree does the increased variety of parties comprised within the Union, increase this security. Does it, in fine, consist in the greater obstacles opposed to the concert and accomplishment of the secret wishes of an unjust and interested majority? Here, again, the extent of the Union gives it the most palpable advantage.

The influence of factious leaders may kindle a flame within their particular states, but will be unable to spread a general conflagration through the other states. A religious sect may degenerate into a political faction in a part of the Confederacy; but the variety of sects dispersed over the entire face of it must secure the national councils against any danger from that source. A rage for paper money, for an abolition of debts, for an equal division of property, or for any other improper or wicked project, will be less apt to pervade the whole body of the Union than a particular member of it; in the same proportion as such a malady is more likely to taint a particular county or district, than an entire state. In the extent and proper structure of the Union, therefore, we behold a republican remedy for the diseases most incident to republican government. And according to the degree of pleasure and pride we feel in being republicans, ought to be our zeal in cherishing the spirit and supporting the character of Federalists.

PUBLIUS.

LETTER BY JOHN ADAMS TO THOMAS JEFFERSON

("... elections to offices which are great objects
of ambition, I look at with terror")

LONDON
DECEMBER 6, 1787

> *Two of America's most important men were not in the United States
> at the time of the Convention. John Adams (1735–1826), the coun-
> try's Ambassador to Great Britain, was in London and Thomas Jef-
> ferson (1743–1826), serving as United States Minister to France,
> was in Paris. As an author and politician, Adams had already influ-
> enced the constitutions of several states and had written that of his
> home state of Massachusetts. He would become the second President
> of the United States.*

Dear Sir,

The project of a new Constitution has objections against it, to
which I find it difficult to reconcile myself, but I am so unfortunate
as to differ somewhat from you in the articles, according to your last
kind letter.

You are afraid of the one—I, of the few. We agree perfectly that
the many should have a full fair and perfect representation.—You
are apprehensive of monarchy; I, of aristocracy.—I would therefore
have given more power to the President and less to the Senate. The
nomination and appointment to all offices I would have given to the
President, assisted only by a Privy Council of his own appointment
creation, but not a vote or voice would I have given to the Senate or
any Senator, unless he were of the Privy Council. Faction and distrac-
tion are the sure and certain consequence of giving to a Senate a vote
in the distribution of offices.

You are apprehensive the President when once chosen will be
chosen again and again as long as he lives. So much the better as it

appears to me.—You are apprehensive of foreign interference, intrigue, influence.—So am I.—But, as often as elections happen, the danger of foreign influence recurs. The less frequently they happen the less danger.—And if the same man may be chosen again, it is probable he will be, and the danger of foreign influence will be less. Foreigners, seeing little prospect will have less courage for enterprise.

Elections, my dear sir, elections to offices which are great objects of ambition, I look at with terror.—Experiments of this kind have been so often tried, and so universally found productive of horrors, that there is great reason to dread them.

Mr. Littlepage, who will have the honor to deliver this, will tell you all the news.

I am, etc. etc.

LETTER BY THOMAS JEFFERSON
TO JAMES MADISON

("...a bill of rights is what the people are entitled
to against every government on earth ...")

DECEMBER 20, 1787
PARIS

*When he received the Constitution by mail in November of 1787,
the author of the Declaration of Independence was distressed by various points. In the first paragraph, Jefferson catches up on and responds
to personal matters, after which he introduces the important and considered thoughts he has had about Madison's great project. Jefferson
would serve as the country's first Secretary of State and in 1800 was
elected the third President of the United States.*

Dear Sir,

My last to you was of October the 8th, by the Count de Moustier.
Yours of July the 18th, September the 6th, and October the 24th, were
successively received, yesterday, the day before, and three or four days
before that. I have only had time to read the letters; the printed papers
communicated with them, however interesting, being obliged to lie
over till I finish my dispatches for the packet, which dispatches must
go from hence the day after tomorrow. I have much to thank you for:
first and most for the ciphered paragraph respecting myself. These little
informations are very material towards forming my own decisions. I
would be glad even to know, when any individual member thinks I
have gone wrong in any instance. If I know myself, it would not excite
ill blood in me, while it would assist to guide my conduct, perhaps to
justify it, and to keep me to my duty, alert. I must thank you, too, for
the information in Thomas Burke's case; though you will have found
by a subsequent letter, that I have asked of you a further investigation
of that matter. It is to gratify the lady who is at the head of the convent
wherein my daughters are, and who, by her attachment and attention

to them, lays me under great obligations, I shall hope, therefore, still to receive from you the result of all the further inquiries my second letter had asked. The parcel of rice which you informed me had miscarried, accompanied my letter to the Delegates of South Carolina. Mr. Bourgoin was to be the bearer of both, and both were delivered together into the hands of his relation here, who introduced him to me, and who, at a subsequent moment, undertook to convey them to Mr. Bourgoin. This person was an engraver, particularly recommended to Dr. Franklin and Mr. Hopkinson. Perhaps he may have mislaid the little parcel of rice among his baggage. I am much pleased, that the sale of western lands is so successful. I hope they will absorb all the certificates of our domestic debt speedily, in the first place, and that then, offered for cash, they will do the same by our foreign ones.

The season admitting only of operations in the cabinet, and these being in a great measure secret, I have little to fill a letter, I will therefore make up the deficiency, by adding a few words on the constitution proposed by our convention.

I like much the general idea of framing a government, which should go on of itself, peaceably, without needing continual recurrence to the state legislatures. I like the organization of the government into legislative, judiciary, and executive. I like the power given the legislature to levy taxes, and for that reason solely, I approve of the greater House being chosen by the people directly. For though I think a House, so chosen, will be very far inferior to the present Congress, will be very illy qualified to legislate for the Union, for foreign nations, etc.; yet this evil does not weigh against the good of preserving inviolate the fundamental principle, that the people are not to be taxed but by representatives chosen immediately by themselves. I am captivated by the compromise of the opposite claims of the great and little states, of the latter to equal, and the former to proportional influence. I am much pleased, too, with the substitution of the method of voting by persons, instead of that of voting by states: and I like the negative given to the executive, conjointly with a third of either house; though I should have liked it better, had the judiciary been associated for that purpose, or invested separately with a similar power. There are other good things of less moment.

I will now tell you what I do not like. First, the omission of a bill of rights, providing clearly, and without the aid of sophism, for freedom of religion, freedom of the press, protection against standing armies, restriction of monopolies, the eternal and unremitting force of the *habeas corpus* laws, and trials by jury in all matters of fact triable by the laws of the land, and not by the laws of nations. To say, as Mr. Wilson does, that a bill of rights was not necessary, because all is reserved in the case of the general government which is not given, while in the particular ones, all is given which is not reserved, might do for the audience to which it was addressed: but it is surely a *gratis dictum*, the reverse of which might just as well be said; and it is opposed by strong inferences from the body of the instrument, as well as from the omission of the clause of our present Confederation, which had made the reservation in express terms. It was hard to conclude, because there has been a want of uniformity among the states as to the cases triable by jury, because some have been so incautious as to dispense with this mode of trial in certain cases, therefore the more prudent states shall be reduced to the same level of calamity. It would have been much more just and wise to have concluded the other way, that as most of the states had preserved with jealousy this sacred palladium of liberty, those who had wandered, should be brought back to it: and to have established general right rather than general wrong. For I consider all the ill as established, which may be established. I have a right to nothing, which another has a right to take away; and Congress will have a right to take away trials by jury in all civil cases. Let me add, that a bill of rights is what the people are entitled to against every government on earth, general or particular; and what no just government should refuse, or rest on inference.

The second feature I dislike, and strongly dislike, is the abandonment, in every instance, of the principle of rotation in office, and most particularly in the case of the President. Reason and experience tell us, that the first magistrate will always be re-elected if he may be re-elected. He is then an officer for life.

This once observed, it becomes of so much consequence to certain nations, to have a friend or a foe at the head of our affairs, that they will interfere with money and with arms. A Galloman, or an Angloman, will be supported by the nation he befriends. If once elected, and at a second or third election outvoted by one or two votes, he will pretend false votes, foul play, hold possession of the reins of government, be supported by the states voting for him, especially if they be the central ones, lying in a compact body themselves, and separating their opponents; and they will be aided by one nation in Europe, while the majority are aided by another. The election of a President of America, some years hence, will be much more interesting to certain nations of Europe, than ever the election of a King of Poland was. Reflect on all the instances in history, ancient and modern, of elective monarchies, and say, if they do not give foundation for my fears; the Roman emperors, the popes while they were of any importance, the German emperors till they became hereditary in practice, the Kings of Poland, the deys of the Ottoman dependencies. It may be said, that if elections are to be attended with these disorders, the less frequently they are repeated the better. But experience says, that to free them from disorder, they must be rendered less interesting by a necessity of change. No foreign power, nor domestic party, will waste their blood and money to elect a person, who must go out at the end of a short period. The power of removing every fourth year by the vote of the people, is a power which they will not exercise, and if they were disposed to exercise it, they would not be permitted. The King of Poland is removable every day by the diet. But they never remove him. Nor would Russia, the emperor, etc., permit them to do it. Smaller objections are, the appeals on matters of fact as well as law; and the binding all persons, legislative, executive, and judiciary, by oath, to maintain that constitution. I do not pretend to decide, what would be the best method of procuring the establishment of the manifold good things in this constitution, and of getting rid of the bad. Whether by adopting it, in hopes of future amendment; or, after it shall have been duly weighed and canvassed by the people, after seeing the parts they generally dislike, and those they generally approve, to say to them, "We see now what you wish. You are willing to give to your federal government such and such powers: but you wish, at the same time, to have such and such fundamental rights secured to you, and certain sources of convulsion taken away. Be it so. Send together your deputies again. Let them establish your fundamental rights by a sacrosanct declaration, and let them pass the parts of the constitution you have approved. These will give powers to your federal government sufficient for your happiness." This is what might be said, and would probably produce a speedy, more perfect, and more permanent form of government. At all events, I hope you will not be discouraged from making other trials, if the present one should fail. We are never permitted to despair of the commonwealth.

I have thus told you freely what I like, and what I dislike, merely as a matter of curiosity; for I know it is not in my power to offer matter of information to your judgment, which has been formed after hearing and weighing every thing which the wisdom of man could offer on these subjects. I own, I am not a friend to a very energetic government. It is always oppressive. It places the governors indeed more at their ease, at the expense of the people. The late rebellion in Massachusetts has given more alarm, than I think it should have done. Calculate that one rebellion in thirteen states in the course of eleven years, is but one for each state in a century and a half. No country should be so long without one. Nor will any degree of power in the hands of government prevent insurrections. In England, where the hand of power is heavier than with us, there are seldom half a dozen years without an insurrection. In France, where it is still heavier, but less despotic, as Montesquieu supposes, than in some other countries, and where there are always two or three hundred thousand men ready to crush insurrections, there have been three in the course of the three years I have been here, in every one of which greater numbers were engaged than in Massachusetts, and a great deal more blood was spilt. In Turkey, where the sole nod of the despot is death, insurrections are the events of every day. Compare again the ferocious depredations of their insurgents, with the order, the moderation, and the almost self-extinguishment of ours. And say, finally, whether peace is best preserved by giving energy to the government, or information to the people. This last is the most certain and the most legitimate engine of government.

Educate and inform the whole mass of the people. Enable them to see that it is their interest to preserve peace and order, and they will preserve them. And it requires no very high degree of education to convince them of this. They are the only sure reliance for the preservation of our liberty. After all, it is my principle that the will of the majority should prevail. If they approve the proposed constitution in all its parts, I shall concur in it cheerfully, in hopes they will amend it, whenever they shall find it works wrong. This reliance cannot deceive us, as long as we remain virtuous; and I think we shall be so, as long as agriculture is our principal object, which will be the case, while there remain vacant lands in any part of America. When we get piled upon one another in large cities, as in Europe, we shall become corrupt as in Europe, and go to eating one another as they do there. I have tired you by this time with disquisitions which you have already heard repeated by others, a thousand and a thousand times; and, therefore, shall only add assurances of the esteem and attachment, with which I have the honor to be, Dear Sir, your affectionate friend and servant,

Th: Jefferson

P. S. The instability of our laws is really an immense evil. I think it would be well to provide in our constitutions, that there shall always be a twelvemonth between the engrossing a bill and passing it: that it should then be offered to its passage without changing a word: and that if circumstances should be thought to require a speedier passage, it should take two thirds of both houses, instead of a bare majority.

DEBATE IN THE MASSACHUSETTS RATIFYING CONVENTION: AMOS SINGLETARY AND JONATHAN B. SMITH

("... I have known the worth of good government by the want of it")

THE CONVENTION OF THE COMMONWEALTH OF MASSACHUSETTS, ON THE ADOPTION OF THE FEDERAL CONSTITUTION
JANUARY 25, 1788

Amos Singletary of Sutton, Worcester County, and Jonathan B. Smith, of Lanesboro, Berkshire County, were members of the Massachusetts Ratifying Convention. On February 6, 1788, Massachusetts ratified the Constitution by a vote of 187–168.

MR. SINGLETARY: Mr. President, I should not have troubled the Convention again, if some gentlemen had not called on them that were on the stage in the beginning of our troubles, in the year 1775. I was one of them. I have had the honor to be a member of the court all the time, Mr. President, and I say that, if any body had proposed such a constitution as this in that day, it would have been thrown away at once. It would not have been looked at. We contended with Great Britain, some said for a three-penny duty on tea; but it was not that; it was because they claimed a right to tax us and bind us in all cases whatever. And does not this Constitution do the same? Does it not take away all we have — all our property? Does it not lay all taxes, duties, imposts, and excises? And what more have we to give? They tell us Congress won't lay dry taxes upon us, but collect all the money they want by impost. I say, there has always been a difficulty about impost. Whenever the General Court was going to lay an impost, they would tell us it was more than trade could bear, that it hurt the fair trader, and encouraged smuggling; and there will always be the same objection: they won't be able to raise money enough by impost, and then they will lay it on the land, and take all we have got.

These lawyers, and men of learning, and moneyed men, that talk so finely, and gloss over matters so smoothly, to make us poor illiterate people swallow down the pill, expect to get into Congress themselves; they expect to be the managers of this Constitution, and get all the power and all the money into their own hands, and then they will swallow up all us little folks, like the great Leviathan, Mr. President; yes, just as the whale swallowed up Jonah. This is what I am afraid of; but I won't say any more at present, but reserve the rest to another opportunity.

MR. SMITH: Mr. President, I am a plain man, and get my living by the plough. I am not used to speak in public, but I beg your leave to say a few words to my brother plough-joggers in this house. I have lived in a part of the country where I have known the worth of good government by the want of it.

There was a black cloud that rose in the east last winter, and spread over the west. (*Here MR. WIDGERY interrupted: "Mr. President, I wish to know what the gentleman means by 'the east.'"*) I mean, sir, the county of Bristol; the cloud rose there, and burst upon us, and produced a dreadful effect. It brought on a state of anarchy, and that led to tyranny. I say, it brought anarchy. People that used to live peaceably, and were before good neighbors, got distracted, and took up arms against government. (*Here MR. KINGSLEY called to order, and asked, what had the history of last winter to do with the Constitution. Several gentlemen, and among the rest the Hon. Mr. Adams, said the gentleman was in order—let him go on in his own way.*) I am going, Mr. President, to show you, my brother farmers, what were the effects of anarchy, that you may see the reasons why I wish for good government. People I say took up arms; and then, if you went to speak to them, you had the musket of death presented to your breast. They would rob you of your property; threaten to burn your houses; oblige you to be on your guard night and day; alarms spread from town to town; families were broken up; the tender mother would cry, "O, my son is among them! What shall I do for my child!" Some were taken captive, children taken out of their schools, and carried away.

Then we should hear of an action, and the poor prisoners were set in the front, to be killed by their own friends. How dreadful, how distressing was this! Our distress was so great that we should have been glad to snatch at any thing that looked like a government. Had any person, that was able to protect us, come and set up his standard, we should all have flocked to it, even if it had been a monarch; and that monarch might have proved a tyrant;—so that you see that anarchy leads to tyranny, and better have one tyrant than so many at once.

Now, Mr. President, when I saw this Constitution, I found that it was a cure for these disorders. It was just such a thing as we wanted. I got a copy of it, and read it over and over. I had been a member of the Convention to form our own state constitution, and had learnt something of the checks and balances of power, and I found them all here. I did not go to any lawyer, to ask his opinion; we have no lawyer in our town, and we do well enough without. I formed my own opinion, and was pleased with this Constitution.

My honorable old daddy there (*pointing to Mr. Singletary*) won't think that I expect to be a Congressman, and swallow up the liberties of the people. I never had any post, nor do I want one. But I don't think the worse of the Constitution because lawyers, and men of learning, and moneyed men, are fond of it. I don't suspect that they want to get into Congress and abuse their power. I am not of such a jealous make. They that are honest men themselves are not apt to suspect other people. I don't know why our constituents have not a good right to be as jealous of us as we seem to be of the Congress; and I think those gentlemen, who are so very suspicious that as soon as a man gets into power he turns rogue, had better look at home.

We are, by this Constitution, allowed to send ten members to Congress. Have we not more than that number fit to go? I dare say, if we pick out ten, we shall have another ten left, and I hope ten times ten; and will not these be a check upon those that go? Will they go to Congress, and abuse their power, and do mischief, when they know they must return and look the other ten in the face, and be called to account for their conduct? Some gentlemen think that our liberty and property are not safe in the hands of moneyed men, and men of learning? I am not of that mind.

Brother farmers, let us suppose a case, now: Suppose you had a farm of 50 acres, and your title was disputed, and there was a farm of 5,000 acres joined to you, that belonged to a man of learning, and his title was involved in the same difficulty; would you not be glad to have him for your friend, rather than to stand alone in the dispute? Well, the case is the same. These lawyers, these moneyed men, these men of learning, are all embarked in the same cause with us, and we must all swim or sink together; and shall we throw the Constitution overboard because it does not please us alike? Suppose two or three of you had been at the pains to break up a piece of rough land, and sow it with wheat; would you let it lie waste because you could not agree what sort of a fence to make? Would it not be better to put up a fence that did not please every one's fancy, rather than not fence it at all, or keep disputing about it until the wild beasts came in and devoured it? Some gentlemen say, Don't be in a hurry; take time to consider, and don't take a leap in the dark. I say, Take things in time; gather fruit when it is ripe. There is a time to sow and a time to reap; we sowed our seed when we sent men to the federal Convention; now is the harvest, now is the time to reap the fruit of our labor; and if we won't do it now, I am afraid we never shall have another opportunity.

DEBATE IN THE MASSACHUSETTS RATIFYING CONVENTION: SPEECH BY NATHANIEL BARRELL

("... excellent as this system is, in some respects it needs alterations ...")

THE CONVENTION OF THE COMMONWEALTH OF MASSACHUSETTS, ON THE ADOPTION OF THE FEDERAL CONSTITUTION FEBRUARY 5, 1788

Against ratification when elected to the Massachusetts convention, Nathaniel Barrell (1732–1831), a businessman from the Maine district of the state, changed his mind.

Awed in the presence of this august assembly—conscious of my inability to express my mind fully on this important occasion and sensible how little I must appear in the eyes of those giants in rhetoric, who have exhibited such a pompous display of declamation—without any of those talents calculated to draw attention, without the pleasing eloquence of Cicero, or the blaze of Demosthenian oratory, I rise, sir, to discharge my duty to my constituents, who I know expect something more from me than merely silent vote. With no pretensions to talents above the simple language adapted to the line of my calling, the plain husbandman, I hope the gentlemen who compose this honorable body will fully understand me when I attempt to speak my mind of the Federal Constitution as it now stands. I wish, sir, to give my voice for its amendment before it can be salutary for our acceptance:

Because, sir, notwithstanding the Wilsonian oratory and all the learned arguments I have seen written notwithstanding the many labored speeches I have heard in its defense, and after the best investigation, I am able to give this subject, I fear it is pregnant with baneful effects, although I may not live to feel them.

Because, sir, as it now stands, Congress will be vested with more extensive powers than ever Great Britain exercised over us, too great in my opinion to entrust with any class of men, let their talents or virtues

114

be ever so conspicuous, even though composed of such exalted ami-
able characters as the great Washington. For while we consider them as
men of like passions, the same spontaneous, inherent thirst for power
with ourselves—great and good as they may be, when they enter
upon this all-important charge, what security can we have that they
will continue so? And, sir, were we sure they would continue the faithful guardians of our liberties, and prevent any infringement on the
privileges of the people, what assurance can we have that such men
will always hold the reins of government—that their successors will
be such? History tells us Rome was happy under Augustus—though
wretched under Nero, who could have no greater power than Augustus—and yet this same Nero, when young in government, could shed
tears on signing a death warrant, though afterwards became so callous
to the tender feelings of humanity as to behold with pleasure Rome
in flames.

Because, sir, I think that six years is too long a term for any set of
men to be at the helm of government. For in that time they may get
so firmly rooted, and their influence be so great as to continue themselves for life.

Because, sir, I am not certain we are able to support the additional
expense of such a government.

Because, sir, I think a Continental collector will not be so likely to do
us justice in collecting the taxes, as collectors of our own.

Because, sir, I think a frame of government on which all laws are
founded, should be so simple and explicit, that the most illiterate may
understand it, whereas this appears to me so obscure and ambiguous
that the most capacious mind cannot fully comprehend it.

Because, sir, the duties of excise and impost, and to be taxed besides,
appears too great a sacrifice—and when we have given them up, what
shall we have to pay our own debts, but a dry tax?

Because, sir, I do not think this will produce the efficient government
we are in pursuit of.

Because, sir, they fix their own salaries without allowing any
control.

And *because, sir,* I think such a government may be disagreeable to
men with the high notions of liberty we Americans have.

And, sir, I could wish this Constitution had not been in some parts
of the continent hurried on like the driving of Jehu very furiously, for
such important transactions should be without force, and with cool
deliberation. These, sir, and those of _____ were my objections, my
constituents, as they occur to my memory some of which have been
removed in the course of the debates, by the ingenious reasonings
of the speakers—I wish I could say the whole were. But after all,

there are some that yet remain on my mind, enough to convince me, excellent as this system is, in some respects it needs alterations; therefore I think it becomes us as wise men, as the faithful guardians of the people's rights, and as we wish well to posterity to propose such amendments as will secure to us and ours that liberty without which life is a burthen.

Thus, sir, have I ventured to deliver my sentiments, in which is involved those of my constituents, on this important subject, cautiously avoiding everything like metaphysical reasoning, least I should invade the prerogative of those respectable gentlemen of the law who have so copiously displayed their talents on this occasion. But, sir, although you may perceive by what I have said, that this is not in my view the most perfect system I could wish, yet as I am possessed with an assurance that the proposed amendments will take place, as I dread the fatal effects of anarchy, as I am convinced the Confederation is essentially deficient, and that it will be more difficult to amend that, than to reform this, and as I think this Constitution with all its imperfections is excellent compared with that, and that it is the best Constitution we can now obtain, as the greatest good I can do my country at present, I could wish for an adjournment, that I might have an opportunity to lay it before my constituents with the arguments which have been used in the debates, which have eased my mind, and I trust would have the effect on theirs, so as heartily to join me in ratifying the same. But, sir, if I cannot be indulged on this desirable object, I am almost tempted to risk their displeasure and adopt it without their consent.

ARTICLE, *THE FEDERALIST*, NO. 51, "THE STRUCTURE OF THE GOVERNMENT MUST FURNISH THE PROPER CHECKS AND BALANCES BETWEEN THE DIFFERENT DEPARTMENTS," BY JAMES MADISON

("If men were angels, no government would be necessary")

FEBRUARY 6, 1788

No one believed as deeply in the ultimate and practical benefits of the Constitution as James Madison. His knowledge of its strengths and weaknesses allowed him to maintain continuous explications of and arguments for it.

To the People of the State of New York:

To what expedient, then, shall we finally resort, for maintaining in practice the necessary partition of power among the several departments, as laid down in the Constitution? The only answer that can be given is, that as all these exterior provisions are found to be inadequate, the defect must be supplied, by so contriving the interior structure of the government as that its several constituent parts may, by their mutual relations, be the means of keeping each other in their proper places. Without presuming to undertake a full development of this important idea, I will hazard a few general observations, which may perhaps place it in a clearer light, and enable us to form a more correct judgment of the principles and structure of the government planned by the convention.

In order to lay a due foundation for that separate and distinct exercise of the different powers of government, which to a certain extent is admitted on all hands to be essential to the preservation of liberty, it is evident that each department should have a will of its own; and consequently should be so constituted that the members of each should have as little agency as possible in the appointment of the members of the others. Were this principle rigorously adhered to, it would require that all the appointments for the supreme executive, legislative, and judiciary magistracies should be drawn from the same fountain of authority, the people, through channels having no communication whatever with one another. Perhaps such a plan of constructing the several departments would be less difficult in practice than it may in contemplation appear. Some difficulties, however, and some additional expense would attend the execution of it. Some deviations, therefore, from the principle must be admitted. In the constitution of the judiciary department in particular, it might be inexpedient to insist rigorously on the principle: first, because peculiar qualifications being essential in the members, the primary consideration ought to be to select that mode of choice which best secures these qualifications; secondly, because the permanent tenure by which the appointments are held in that department, must soon destroy all sense of dependence on the authority conferring them.

It is equally evident, that the members of each department should be as little dependent as possible on those of the others, for the emoluments annexed to their offices. Were the executive magistrate, or the judges, not independent of the legislature in this particular, their independence in every other would be merely nominal.

But the great security against a gradual concentration of the several powers in the same department, consists in giving to those who administer each department the necessary constitutional means and personal motives to resist encroachments of the others. The provision for defense must in this, as in all other cases, be made commensurate to the danger of attack. Ambition must be made to counteract ambition. The interest of the man must be connected with the constitutional rights of the place. It may be a reflection on human nature, that such devices should be necessary to control the abuses of government. But what is government itself, but the greatest of all reflections on human nature? If men were angels, no government would be necessary. If angels were to govern men, neither external nor internal controls on government would be necessary. In framing a government which is to be administered by men over men, the great difficulty lies in this: you must first enable the government to control the governed; and in the next place oblige it to control itself. A dependence on the people is, no doubt, the primary control on the government; but experience has taught mankind the necessity of auxiliary precautions.

This policy of supplying, by opposite and rival interests, the defect of better motives, might be traced through the whole system of human affairs, private as well as public. We see it particularly displayed in all the subordinate distributions of power, where the constant aim is to divide and arrange the several offices in such a manner as that each may be a check on the other that the private interest of every individual may be a sentinel over the public rights. These inventions of prudence cannot be less requisite in the distribution of the supreme powers of the state.

But it is not possible to give to each department an equal power of self-defense. In republican government, the legislative authority necessarily predominates. The remedy for this inconveniency is to divide the legislature into different branches; and to render them, by different modes of election and different principles of action, as little connected with each other as the nature of their common functions and their common dependence on the society will admit. It may even be necessary to guard against dangerous encroachments by still further precautions. As the weight of the legislative authority requires that it should be thus divided, the weakness of the executive may require, on the other hand, that it should be fortified. An absolute negative on the legislature appears, at first view, to be the natural defense with which the executive magistrate should be armed. But perhaps it would be neither altogether safe nor alone sufficient. On ordinary occasions it might not be exerted with the requisite firmness, and on extraordinary occasions it might be perfidiously abused. May not this defect of an absolute negative be supplied by some qualified connection between this weaker department and the weaker branch of the stronger department, by which the latter may be led to support the constitutional rights of the former, without being too much detached from the rights of its own department?

If the principles on which these observations are founded be just, as I persuade myself they are, and they be applied as a criterion to the several state constitutions, and to the federal Constitution it will be found that if the latter does not perfectly correspond with them, the former are infinitely less able to bear such a test.

There are, moreover, two considerations particularly applicable to the federal system of America, which place that system in a very interesting point of view.

First. In a single republic, all the power surrendered by the people is submitted to the administration of a single government; and the usurpations are guarded against by a division of the government into distinct and separate departments. In the compound republic of America, the power surrendered by the people is first divided between two distinct governments, and then the portion allotted to each subdivided among distinct and separate departments. Hence a double security arises to the rights of the people. The different governments will control each other, at the same time that each will be controlled by itself.

Second. It is of great importance in a republic not only to guard the society against the oppression of its rulers, but to guard one part of the society against the injustice of the other part. Different interests necessarily exist in different classes of citizens. If a majority be united by a common interest, the rights of the minority will be insecure. There are but two methods of providing against this evil: the one by creating a will in the community independent of the majority that is, of the society itself; the other, by comprehending in the society so many separate descriptions of citizens as will render an unjust combination of a majority of the whole very improbable, if not impracticable. The first method prevails in all governments possessing an hereditary or self-appointed authority. This, at best, is but a precarious security; because a power independent of the society may as well espouse the unjust views of the major, as the rightful interests of the minor party, and may possibly be turned against both parties. The second method will be exemplified in the federal republic of the United States. Whilst all authority in it will be derived from and dependent on the society, the society itself will be broken into so many parts, interests, and classes of citizens, that the rights of individuals, or of the minority, will be in little danger from interested combinations of the majority. In a free government the security for civil rights must be the same as that for religious rights. It consists in the one case in the multiplicity of interests, and in the other in the multiplicity of sects. The degree of security in both cases will depend on the number of interests and sects; and this may be presumed to depend on the extent of country and number of people comprehended under the same government. This view of the subject must particularly recommend a proper federal system to all the sincere and considerate friends of republican government, since it shows that in exact proportion as the territory of the Union may be formed into more circumscribed Confederacies, or states oppressive combinations of a majority will be facilitated: the best security, under the republican forms, for the rights of every class of citizens, will be diminished: and consequently the stability and independence of some member of the government, the only other security, must be proportionately increased. Justice is the end of government. It is the end of civil society. It ever has been and ever will be pursued until it be obtained, or until liberty be lost in the pursuit. In a society under the forms of which the stronger faction can readily unite and oppress the weaker, anarchy may as truly be said to reign as in a state of nature, where the weaker individual is not secured against the violence of the stronger; and as, in the latter state, even the stronger individuals are prompted, by the uncertainty of their condition, to submit to a government which may protect the weak as well as themselves; so, in the former state, will the more powerful factions or parties be gradually induced, by a like motive, to wish for a government which will protect all parties, the weaker as well as the more powerful. It can be little doubted that if the state of Rhode Island was separated from the Confederacy and left to itself, the insecurity of rights under the popular form of government within such narrow limits would be displayed by such reiterated oppressions of factious majorities that some power altogether independent of the people would soon be called for by the voice of the very factions whose misrule had proved the necessity of it. In the extended republic of the United States, and among the great variety of interests, parties, and sects which it embraces, a coalition of a majority of the whole society could seldom take place on any other principles than those of justice and the general good; whilst there being thus less danger to a minor from the will of a major party, there must be less pretext, also, to provide for the security of the former, by introducing into the government a will not dependent on the latter, or, in other words, a will independent of the society itself. It is no less certain than it is important, notwithstanding the contrary opinions which have been entertained, that the larger the society, provided it lie within a practical sphere, the more duly capable it will be of self-government. And happily for the *republican cause,* the practicable sphere may be carried to a very great extent, by a judicious modification and mixture of the *federal principle*.

PUBLIUS.

ADDRESS TO THE PEOPLE OF THE STATE OF NEW YORK BY JOHN JAY, "A CITIZEN OF NEW YORK"

("Suppose this plan to be rejected; what measures
would you propose for obtaining a better?")

March–April, 1788

John Adams, reflecting on the battle for ratification, believed that John Jay (1745–1829) "had as much influence in the preparatory measures in digesting the Constitution, and obtaining its adoption, as any man in the nation." This essay, published as a pamphlet, takes in more topics more comprehensively than any of the five articles Jay wrote for The Federalist. *At the time, Jay was Secretary for Foreign Affairs for the United States. He would become the first Chief Justice of the Supreme Court in 1789.*

Friends And Fellow-Citizens: The Convention concurred in opinion with the people, that a national government, competent to every national object, was indispensably necessary; and it was as plain to them, as it now is to all America, that the present Confederation does not provide for such a government. These points being agreed, they proceeded to consider how and in what manner such a government could be formed, as, on the one hand, should be sufficiently energetic to raise us from our prostrate and distressed situation, and, on the other, be perfectly consistent with the liberties of the people of every state. Like men to whom the experience of other ages and countries had taught wisdom, they not only determined that it should be erected by, and depend on, the people, but, remembering the many instances in which governments vested solely in one man, or one body of men, had degenerated into tyrannies, they judged it most prudent that the three great branches of power should be committed to different hands, and therefore that the executive should be separated from the legislative, and the judicial from both. Thus far the propriety of their work is easily seen and understood, and therefore is thus far almost universally approved; for no one man or thing under the sun ever yet pleased every body.

The next question was, what particular powers should be given to these three branches. Here the different views and interests of the different states, as well as the different abstract opinions of their members on such points, interposed many difficulties. Here the business became complicated, and presented a wide field for investigation—too wide for every eye to take a quick and comprehensive view of it.

It is said that "in a multitude of counselors there is safety," because, in the first place, there is greater security for probity; and in the next, if every member cast in only his mite of information and argument, their joint stock of both will thereby become greater than the stock possessed by any one single man out of doors. Gentlemen out of doors, therefore, should not be hasty in condemning a system which probably rests on more good reasons than they are aware of, especially when formed under such advantages, and recommended by so many men of distinguished worth and abilities.

The difficulties before mentioned occupied the Convention a long time; and it was not without mutual concessions that they were at last surmounted. These concessions serve to explain to us the reason why some parts of the system please in some states which displease in others, and why many of the objections which have been made to it are so contradictory and inconsistent with one another. It does great credit to the temper and talents of the Convention, that they were able so to reconcile the different views and interests of the different states, and the clashing opinions of their members, as to unite with such singular and almost perfect unanimity in any plan whatever, on a subject so intricate and perplexed. It shows that it must have been thoroughly discussed and understood; and probably, if the community at large had the same lights and reasons before them, they would, if equally candid and uninfluenced, be equally unanimous.

It would be arduous, and indeed impossible, to comprise within the limits of this address a full discussion of every part of the plan. Such a task would require a volume; and few men have leisure or inclination to read volumes on any subject. The objections made to it are almost without number, and many of them without reason. Some of them are real and honest, and others merely ostensible. There are friends to union and a national government who have serious doubts, who wish to be informed, and to be convinced; and there are others, who, neither wishing for union nor any national government at all, will oppose and object to any plan that can be contrived.

We are told, among other strange things, that the liberty of the press is left insecure by the proposed Constitution; and yet that Constitution says neither more nor less about it than the Constitution of the state of New York does. We are told that it deprives us of trial by jury; whereas the fact is, that it expressly secures it in certain cases, and takes it away in none. It is absurd to construe the silence of this, or of our own Constitution, relative to a great number of our rights, into a total extinction of them. Silence and blank paper neither grant nor take away any thing. Complaints are also made that the proposed Constitution is not accompanied by a bill of rights; and yet they who make these complaints know, and are content, that no bill of rights accompanied the Constitution of this state. In days and countries where monarchs and their subjects were frequently disputing about prerogative and privileges, the latter then found it necessary, as it were, to run out the line between them, and oblige the former to admit, by solemn acts, called bills of rights, that certain enumerated rights belonged to the people, and were not comprehended in the royal prerogative. But, thank God, we have no such disputes; we have no monarchs to contend with, or demand admissions from. The proposed government is to be the government of the people: all its officers are to be their officers, and to exercise no rights but such as the people commit to them. The Constitution only serves to point out that part of the people's business, which they think proper by it to refer to the management of the persons therein designated: those persons are to receive that business to manage, not for themselves, and as their own, but as agents and overseers for the people, to whom they are constantly responsible, and by whom only they are to be appointed.

But the design of this address is not to investigate the merits of the plan, nor of the objections made to it. They who seriously contemplate the present state of our affairs, will be convinced that other considerations, of at least equal importance, demand their attention. Let it be admitted that this plan, like every thing else devised by man, has its imperfections. That it does not please every body, is certain; and there is little reason to expect one that will. It is a question of great moment to you, whether the probability of our being able seasonably to obtain a better, is such as to render it prudent and advisable to reject this, and run the risk. Candidly to consider this question, is the design of this address.

As the importance of this question must be obvious to every man, whatever his private opinions respecting it may be, it becomes us all to treat it in that calm and temperate manner which a subject so deeply interesting to the future welfare of our country, and prosperity, requires. Let us, therefore, as much as possible, repress and compose that irritation in our minds which too warm disputes about it may have excited. Let us endeavor to forget that this or that man is on this or that side; and that we ourselves, perhaps without sufficient reflection, have classed ourself with one or the other party. Let us remember that this is not to be regarded as a matter that only touches our local parties, but as one so great, so general, and so extensive, in its future consequence to America, that, for our deciding upon it according to the best of our unbiased judgment, we must be highly responsible both here and hereafter.

The question now before us naturally leads to three inquiries:—

1. Whether it is probable that a better plan can be obtained.

2. Whether, if attainable, it is likely to be in season.

3. What would be our situation if, after rejecting this, all our efforts to obtain a better should prove fruitless.

The men who formed this plan are Americans, who had long deserved and enjoyed our confidence, and who are as much interested in having a good government as any of us are or can be. They were appointed to that business at a time when the states had become very sensible of the derangement of our national affairs, and of the impossibility of retrieving them under the existing Confederation. Although well persuaded that nothing but a good national government could oppose and divert the tide of evils that was flowing in upon us, yet those gentlemen met in Convention with minds perfectly unprejudiced in favor of any particular plan. The minds of their constituents were at that time equally cool and dispassionate. All agreed in the necessity of doing something; but no one ventured to say decidedly what precisely ought to be done. Opinions were then fluctuating and unfixed; and whatever might have been the wishes of a few individuals, yet while the Convention deliberated, the people remained in silent suspense. Neither wedded to favorite systems of their own, nor influenced by popular ones abroad, the members were more desirous to receive light from, than to impress their private sentiments on, one another.

These circumstances naturally opened the door to that spirit of candor, of calm inquiry, of mutual accommodation, and mutual respect, which entered into the Convention with them, and regulated their debates and proceedings.

The impossibility of agreeing upon any plan, that would exactly quadrate with the local policy and objects of every state, soon became evident; and they wisely thought it better mutually to coincide and accommodate, and in that way to fashion their system as much as possible by the circumstances and wishes of the different states, than, by pertinaciously adhering each to his own ideas, oblige the Convention to rise without doing any thing. They were sensible that obstacles, arising from local circumstances, would not cease while those circumstances continued to exist; and, so far as those circumstances depended on differences of climate, productions, and commerce, that no change was to be expected. They were likewise sensible that, on a subject so comprehensive, and involving such a variety of points and questions, the most able, the most candid, and the most honest men will differ in opinion. The same proposition seldom strikes many minds exactly in the same point of light. Different habits of thinking, different degrees and modes of education, different prejudices and opinions, early formed and long entertained, conspire, with a multitude of other circumstances, to produce among men a diversity and contrariety of opinions on questions of difficulty. Liberality, therefore, as well as prudence, induced them to treat each other's opinions with tenderness; to argue without asperity; and to endeavor to convince the judgment, without hurting the feelings, of each other. Although many weeks were passed in these discussions, some points remained on which a unison of opinions could not be effected. Here, again, that same happy disposition to unite and conciliate induced them to meet each other; and enabled them, by mutual concessions, finally to complete and agree to the plan they have recommended, and that, too, with a degree of unanimity which, considering the variety of discordant views and ideas they had to reconcile, is really astonishing.

They tell us, very honestly, that this plan is the result of accommodation. They do not hold it up as the best of all possible ones, but only as the best which they could unite in and agree to. If such men, appointed and meeting under such auspicious circumstances, and so sincerely disposed to conciliation, could go no farther in their endeavors to please every state and every body, what reason have we, at present, to expect any system that would give more general satisfaction?

Suppose this plan to be rejected; what measures would you propose for obtaining a better? Some will answer, "Let us appoint another convention; and, as every thing has been said and written that can well be said and written on the subject, they will be better informed than the former one was, and consequently be better able to make and agree upon a more eligible one."

This reasoning is fair, and, as far as it goes, has weight; but it nevertheless takes one thing for granted which appears very doubtful; for, although the new convention might have more information, and perhaps equal abilities, yet it does not from thence follow that they would be equally disposed to agree. The contrary of this position is most probable. You must have observed that the same temper and equanimity which prevailed among the people on former occasions, no longer exist. We have unhappily become divided into parties; and this important subject has been handled with such indiscreet and offensive acrimony, and with so many little, unhandsome artifices and misrepresentations, that pernicious heats and animosities have been kindled, and spread their flames far and wide among us. When, therefore, it becomes a question who shall be deputed to the new convention, we cannot flatter ourselves that the talents and integrity of the candidates will determine who shall be elected. Federal electors will vote for federal deputies, and anti-federal electors for anti-federal ones. Nor will either party prefer the most moderate of their adherents; for, as the most stanch and active partisans will be the most popular, so the men most willing and able to carry points, to oppose and divide, and embarrass their opponents, will be chosen. A convention formed at such a season, and of such men, would be but too exact an epitome of the great body that named them. The same party views, the same propensity to opposition, the same distrusts and jealousies, and the same unaccommodating spirit, which prevail without, would be concentrated and ferment with still greater violence within. Each deputy would recollect who sent him, and why he was sent, and be too apt to consider himself bound in honor to contend and act vigorously under the standard of his party, and not hazard their displeasure by preferring compromise to victory. As vice does not sow the seed of virtue, so neither does passion cultivate the fruits of reason. Suspicions and resentments create no disposition to conciliate; nor do they infuse a desire of making partial and personal objects bend to general union and the common good. The utmost efforts of that excellent disposition were necessary to enable the late Convention to perform their task; and although contrary causes sometimes operate similar effects, yet to expect that discord and animosity should produce the fruits of confidence and agreement, is to expect "grapes from thorns, and figs from thistles."

The states of Georgia, Delaware, Jersey, and Connecticut, have adopted the present plan with unexampled unanimity. They are content with it as it is; and consequently their deputies, being apprised of the sentiments of their constituents, will be little inclined to make alterations, and cannot be otherwise than averse to changes, which they have no reason to think would be agreeable to their people. Some other states, though less unanimous, have nevertheless adopted it by very respectable majorities — and for reasons so evidently cogent, that even the minority in one of them have nobly pledged themselves for its promotion and support. From these circumstances, the new convention would derive and experience difficulties unknown to the former. Nor are these the only additional difficulties they would have to encounter. Few are ignorant that there has lately sprung up a sect of politicians who teach, and profess to believe, that the extent of our nation is too great for the superintendence of one national government, and on that principle argue that it ought to be divided into two or three. This doctrine, however mischievous in its tendency and consequences, has its advocates; and, should any of them be sent to the convention, it will naturally be their policy rather to cherish than to prevent divisions; for, well knowing that the institution of any national government would blast their favorite system, no measures that lead to it can meet with their aid or approbation.

Nor can we be certain whether or not any, and what, foreign influence would, on such an occasion, be indirectly exerted, nor for what purposes. Delicacy forbids an ample discussion of this question. Thus much may be said without error or offence, viz.: that such foreign nations as desire the prosperity of America, and would rejoice to see her become great and powerful, under the auspices of a government wisely calculated to extend her commerce, to encourage her navigation and marine, and to direct the whole weight of her power and resources as her interest and honor may require, will doubtless be friendly to the union of states, and to the establishment of a government able to perpetuate, protect, and dignify it. Such other foreign nations, if any such there be, who, jealous of our growing importance, and fearful that our commerce and navigation should impair their own, behold our rapid population with regret, and apprehend that the enterprising spirit of our people, when seconded by power and probability of success, may be directed to objects not consistent with their policy or interests, cannot fail to wish that we may continue a weak and a divided people.

These considerations merit much attention; and candid men will judge how far they render it probable that a new convention would be able either to agree in a better plan, or, with tolerable unanimity, in any plan at all. Any plan, forcibly carried, by a slender majority, must expect numerous opponents among the people, who, especially in their present temper, would be more inclined to reject than adopt any system so made and carried. We should, in such a case, again see the press teeming with publications for and against it; for, as the minority would take pains to justify their dissent, so would the majority be industrious to display the wisdom of their proceedings. Hence new divisions, new parties, and new distractions, would ensue; and no one can foresee or conjecture when or how they would terminate.

Let those who are sanguine in their expectations of a better plan from a new convention, also reflect on the delays and risks to which it would expose us. Let them consider whether we ought, by continuing much longer in our present humiliating condition, to give other nations further time to perfect their restrictive systems of commerce, reconcile their own people to them, and to fence, and guard, and strengthen them by all those regulations and contrivances in which a jealous policy is ever fruitful. Let them consider whether we ought to give further opportunities to discord to alienate the hearts of our citizens from one another, and thereby encourage new Cromwells to bold exploits. Are we certain that our foreign creditors will continue patient, and ready to proportion their forbearance to our delays? Are we sure that our distresses, dissensions, and weakness, will neither invite hostility nor insult? If they should, how ill prepared shall we be for defence, without union, without government, without money, and without credit!

It seems necessary to remind you that some time must yet elapse before all the states will have decided on the present plan. If they reject it, some time must also pass before the measure of a new convention can be brought about and generally agreed to. A further space of time will then be requisite to elect their deputies, and send them on to convention. What time they may expend, when met, cannot be divined; and it is equally uncertain how much time the several states may take to deliberate and decide on any plan they may recommend. If adopted, still a further space of time will be necessary to organize and set it in motion. In the mean time, our affairs are daily going on from bad to worse; and it is not rash to say that our distresses are accumulating like compound interest.

But if, for the reasons already mentioned, and others that we cannot now perceive, the new convention, instead of producing a better plan, should give us only a history of their disputes, or should offer us one still less pleasing than the present, where should we be then? The old Confederation has done its best, and cannot help us; and is now so relaxed and feeble, that, in all probability, it would not survive so violent a shock. Then, "To your tents, O Israel!" would be the word. Then, every band of union would be severed. Then, every state would be a little nation, jealous of its neighbors, and anxious to strengthen itself, by foreign alliances, against its former friends. Then farewell to fraternal affection, unsuspecting intercourse, and mutual participation in commerce, navigation, and citizenship. Then would arise mutual restrictions and fears, mutual garrisons and standing armies, and all those dreadful evils which for so many ages plagued England, Scotland, Wales, and Ireland, while they continued disunited, and were played off against each other.

Consider, my fellow citizens, what you are about, before it is too late—consider what in such an event would be your particular case.—You know the geography of your state, and the consequences of your local position. Jersey and Connecticut, to whom you imposed laws have been unkind—Jersey and Connecticut, who have adopted the present plan, and expect much good from it, will impute its miscarriage and all the consequent evils to you. They now consider your opposition as dictated more by your fondness for your impost than for those rights to which they have never been behind you in attachment. They cannot, they will not love you—they border upon you, and are your neighbors, but you will soon cease to regard their neighborhood as a blessing. You have but one port and outlet to your commerce, and how you are to keep that outlet free and uninterrupted merits consideration. What advantages Vermont, in combination with others, might take of you, may easily be conjectured; nor will you be at a loss to perceive how much reason the people of Long Island, whom you cannot protect, have to deprecate being constantly exposed to the depredations of every invader.

There are short hints—they ought not to be more developed—you can easily in your own minds dilate and trace them through all their relative circumstances and connections. Pause then for a moment and reflect whether the matters you are disputing about are of sufficient moment to justify your running such extravagant risks. Reflect that the present plan comes recommended to you by men and fellow-citizens, who have given you the highest proofs that men can give of their justice, their love for liberty and their country, of their prudence, of their application, and of their talents. They tell you it is the best that they could form, and that, in their opinion, it is necessary to redeem you from those calamities which already begin to be heavy upon us all. You find that not only those men, but others of similar characters, and of whom you have also had very ample experience, advise you to adopt it. You find that whole states concur in the sentiment, and among them are your neighbors; both of whom have shed much blood in the cause of liberty, and have manifested as strong and constant a predilection for a free republication government as any states in the Union, and perhaps in the world. They perceive not those latent mischiefs in it with which some double-sighted politicians endeavor to alarm you. You cannot but be sensible that this plan or Constitution will always be in the hands and power of the people, and that if on experiment it should be found defective or incompetent, they may either remedy its defects or substitute another in its room. The objectionable parts of it are certainly very questionable, for otherwise there would not be such a contrariety of opinions about them. Experience will better determine such questions than theoretical arguments, and so far as the danger of abuses is urged against the institution of a government, remember that a power to do good always involves a power to do harm. We must in the business of government as well as in all other business have some degree of confidence as well as a great degree of caution. Who on a sick bed would refuse medicines from a physician merely because it as much in his power to administer deadly poison as salutary remedies?

You cannot be certain, that by rejecting the proposed plan you would not place yourselves in a very awkward situation. Suppose nine states should nevertheless adopt it, would you not in that case be obliged either to separate from the Union or rescind your dissent? The first would not be eligible, nor could the latter be pleasant — a mere hint is sufficient on this topic. You cannot but be aware of the consequences.

Consider, then, how weighty and how many considerations advise and persuade the people of America to remain in the safe and easy path of union; to continue to move and act, as they hitherto have done, as a band of brothers; and to have confidence in themselves and in one another; and, since all cannot see with the same eyes, at least to give the proposed Constitution a fair trial, and to mend it as time, occasion, and experience, may dictate. It would little become us to verify the predictions of those who ventured to prophesy that peace, instead of blessing us with happiness and tranquility, would serve only as the signal for factions, discord, and civil contentions, to rage in our land, and overwhelm it with misery and distress.

Let us also be mindful that the cause of freedom greatly depends on the use we make of the singular opportunities we enjoy of governing ourselves wisely; for, if the event should prove that the people of this country either cannot or will not govern themselves, who will hereafter be advocates for systems which, however charming in theory and prospect, are not reducible to practice? If the people of our nation, instead of consenting to be governed by laws of their own making, and rulers of their own choosing, should let licentiousness, disorder, and confusion, reign over them, the minds of men every where will insensibly become alienated from republican forms, and prepared to prefer and acquiesce in governments which, though less friendly to liberty, afford more peace and security.

Receive this address with the same candor with which it is written; and may the spirit of wisdom and patriotism direct and distinguish your councils and your conduct.

ARTICLE, THE *FEDERALIST*, NO. 85, "CONCLUDING REMARKS," BY ALEXANDER HAMILTON

("Let us now pause and ask ourselves whether ... the proposed Constitution has not been satisfactorily vindicated from the aspersions thrown upon it")

MAY 28, 1788

The brilliant and difficult Alexander Hamilton (1755–1804), who had served as George Washington's aide in the Revolutionary War, was the spearhead of The Federalist, *writing fifty-nine of them, with this being the last. He would become the first Secretary of the Treasury, and was the creator of the controversial national bank. He died in a duel with Aaron Burr.*

To the People of the State of New York:

According to the formal division of the subject of these papers, announced in my first number, there would appear still to remain for discussion two points: "the analogy of the proposed government to your own state constitution," and "the additional security which its adoption will afford to republican government, to liberty, and to property." But these heads have been so fully anticipated and exhausted in the progress of the work, that it would now scarcely be possible to do any thing more than repeat, in a more dilated form, what has been heretofore said, which the advanced stage of the question, and the time already spent upon it, conspire to forbid.

It is remarkable, that the resemblance of the plan of the convention to the act which organizes the government of this state holds, not less with regard to many of the supposed defects, than to the real excellences of the former. Among the pretended defects are the re-eligibility of the Executive, the want of a council, the omission of a formal bill of rights, the omission of a provision respecting the liberty of the press. These and several others which have been noted in the course of our inquiries are as much chargeable on the existing constitution of

132

this state, as on the one proposed for the Union; and a man must have slender pretensions to consistency, who can rail at the latter for imperfections which he finds no difficulty in excusing in the former. Nor indeed can there be a better proof of the insincerity and affectation of some of the zealous adversaries of the plan of the convention among us, who profess to be the devoted admirers of the government under which they live, than the fury with which they have attacked that plan, for matters in regard to which our own constitution is equally or perhaps more vulnerable.

The additional securities to republican government, to liberty and to property, to be derived from the adoption of the plan under consideration, consist chiefly in the restraints which the preservation of the Union will impose on local factions and insurrections, and on the ambition of powerful individuals in single states, who may acquire credit and influence enough, from leaders and favorites, to become the despots of the people; in the diminution of the opportunities to foreign intrigue, which the dissolution of the Confederacy would invite and facilitate; in the prevention of extensive military establishments, which could not fail to grow out of wars between the states in a disunited situation; in the express guaranty of a republican form of government to each; in the absolute and universal exclusion of titles of nobility; and in the precautions against the repetition of those practices on the part of the state governments which have undermined the foundations of property and credit, have planted mutual distrust in the breasts of all classes of citizens, and have occasioned an almost universal prostration of morals.

Thus have I, fellow-citizens, executed the task I had assigned to myself; with what success, your conduct must determine. I trust at least you will admit that I have not failed in the assurance I gave you respecting the spirit with which my endeavors should be conducted. I have addressed myself purely to your judgments, and have studiously avoided those asperities which are too apt to disgrace political disputants of all parties, and which have been not a little provoked by the language and conduct of the opponents of the Constitution. The charge of a conspiracy against the liberties of the people, which has been indiscriminately brought against the advocates of the plan, has something in it too wanton and too malignant, not to excite the indignation of every man who feels in his own bosom a refutation of the calumny. The perpetual changes which have been rung upon the wealthy, the well-born, and the great, have been such as to inspire the disgust of all sensible men. And the unwarrantable concealments and misrepresentations which have been in various ways practiced to keep the truth from the public eye, have been of a nature to demand

the reprobation of all honest men. It is not impossible that these circumstances may have occasionally betrayed me into intemperances of
expression which I did not intend; it is certain that I have frequently
felt a struggle between sensibility and moderation; and if the former
has in some instances prevailed, it must be my excuse that it has been
neither often nor much.

Let us now pause and ask ourselves whether, in the course of these
papers, the proposed Constitution has not been satisfactorily vindicated from the aspersions thrown upon it; and whether it has not
been shown to be worthy of the public approbation, and necessary
to the public safety and prosperity. Every man is bound to answer
these questions to himself, according to the best of his conscience and
understanding, and to act agreeably to the genuine and sober dictates
of his judgment. This is a duty from which nothing can give him a
dispensation. 'Tis one that he is called upon, nay, constrained by all the
obligations that form the bands of society, to discharge sincerely and
honestly. No partial motive, no particular interest, no pride of opinion, no temporary passion or prejudice, will justify to himself, to his
country, or to his posterity, an improper election of the part he is to
act. Let him beware of an obstinate adherence to party; let him reflect
that the object upon which he is to decide is not a particular interest
of the community, but the very existence of the nation; and let him
remember that a majority of America has already given its sanction to
the plan which he is to approve or reject.

I shall not dissemble that I feel an entire confidence in the arguments which recommend the proposed system to your adoption, and
that I am unable to discern any real force in those by which it has been
opposed. I am persuaded that it is the best which our political situation, habits, and opinions will admit, and superior to any the revolution has produced.

Concessions on the part of the friends of the plan, that it has not
a claim to absolute perfection, have afforded matter of no small tri-
umph to its enemies. "Why," say they, "should we adopt an imperfect
thing? Why not amend it and make it perfect before it is irrevocably
established?" This may be plausible enough, but it is only plausible.
In the first place I remark, that the extent of these concessions has
been greatly exaggerated. They have been stated as amounting to an
admission that the plan is radically defective, and that without material
alterations the rights and the interests of the community cannot be
safely confided to it. This, as far as I have understood the meaning of
those who make the concessions, is an entire perversion of their sense.
No advocate of the measure can be found, who will not declare as his
sentiment, that the system, though it may not be perfect in every part,

is, upon the whole, a good one; is the best that the present views and circumstances of the country will permit; and is such an one as promises every species of security which a reasonable people can desire.

I answer in the next place, that I should esteem it the extreme of imprudence to prolong the precarious state of our national affairs, and to expose the Union to the jeopardy of successive experiments, in the chimerical pursuit of a perfect plan. I never expect to see a perfect work from imperfect man. The result of the deliberations of all collective bodies must necessarily be a compound, as well of the errors and prejudices, as of the good sense and wisdom, of the individuals of whom they are composed. The compacts which are to embrace thirteen distinct states in a common bond of amity and union, must as necessarily be a compromise of as many dissimilar interests and inclinations. How can perfection spring from such materials?

The reasons assigned in an excellent little pamphlet lately published in this city,[6] are unanswerable to show the utter improbability of assembling a new convention, under circumstances in any degree so favorable to a happy issue, as those in which the late convention met, deliberated, and concluded. I will not repeat the arguments there used, as I presume the production itself has had an extensive circulation. It is certainly well worthy the perusal of every friend to his country. There is, however, one point of light in which the subject of amendments still remains to be considered, and in which it has not yet been exhibited to public view. I cannot resolve to conclude without first taking a survey of it in this aspect.

It appears to me susceptible of absolute demonstration, that it will be far more easy to obtain subsequent than previous amendments to the Constitution. The moment an alteration is made in the present plan, it becomes, to the purpose of adoption, a new one, and must undergo a new decision of each state. To its complete establishment throughout the Union, it will therefore require the concurrence of thirteen states. If, on the contrary, the Constitution proposed should once be ratified by all the states as it stands, alterations in it may at any time be effected by nine states. Here, then, the chances are as thirteen to nine[7] in favor of subsequent amendment, rather than of the original adoption of an entire system.

This is not all. Every Constitution for the United States must inevitably consist of a great variety of particulars, in which thirteen independent states are to be accommodated in their interests or opinions of

---

[6] Entitled "An Address to the People of the State of New York."— *PUBLIUS.*

[7] It may rather be said *ten,* for though two thirds may set on foot the measure, three fourths must ratify. — *PUBLIUS*

interest. We may of course expect to see, in any body of men charged with its original formation, very different combinations of the parts upon different points. Many of those who form a majority on one question, may become the minority on a second, and an association dissimilar to either may constitute the majority on a third. Hence the necessity of moulding and arranging all the particulars which are to compose the whole, in such a manner as to satisfy all the parties to the compact; and hence, also, an immense multiplication of difficulties and casualties in obtaining the collective assent to a final act. The degree of that multiplication must evidently be in a ratio to the number of particulars and the number of parties.

But every amendment to the Constitution, if once established, would be a single proposition, and might be brought forward singly. There would then be no necessity for management or compromise, in relation to any other point no giving nor taking. The will of the requisite number would at once bring the matter to a decisive issue. And consequently, whenever nine, or rather ten states, were united in the desire of a particular amendment, that amendment must infallibly take place. There can, therefore, be no comparison between the facility of affecting an amendment, and that of establishing in the first instance a complete Constitution.

In opposition to the probability of subsequent amendments, it has been urged that the persons delegated to the administration of the national government will always be disinclined to yield up any portion of the authority of which they were once possessed. For my own part I acknowledge a thorough conviction that any amendments which may, upon mature consideration, be thought useful, will be applicable to the organization of the government, not to the mass of its powers; and on this account alone, I think there is no weight in the observation just stated. I also think there is little weight in it on another account. The intrinsic difficulty of governing thirteen states at any rate, independent of calculations upon an ordinary degree of public spirit and integrity, will, in my opinion constantly impose on the national rulers the necessity of a spirit of accommodation to the reasonable expectations of their constituents. But there is yet a further consideration, which proves beyond the possibility of a doubt, that the observation is futile. It is this that the national rulers, whenever nine states concur, will have no option upon the subject. By the fifth article of the plan, the Congress will be obliged "on the application of the legislatures of two thirds of the states, which at present amount to nine, to call a convention for proposing amendments, which shall be valid, to all intents and purposes, as part of the Constitution, when ratified by the legislatures of three fourths of the states, or by conventions in three fourths thereof." The words of this article are peremptory. The Congress "shall call a convention." Nothing in this particular is left to the discretion of that body. And of consequence, all the declamation about the disinclination to a change vanishes in air. Nor however difficult it may be supposed to unite two thirds or three fourths of the state legislatures, in amendments which may affect local interests, can there be any room to apprehend any such difficulty in a union on points which are merely relative to the general liberty or security of the people. We may safely rely on the disposition of the state legislatures to erect barriers against the encroachments of the national authority.

If the foregoing argument is a fallacy, certain it is that I am myself deceived by it, for it is, in my conception, one of those rare instances in which a political truth can be brought to the test of a mathematical demonstration. Those who see the matter in the same light with me, however zealous they may be for amendments, must agree in the propriety of a previous adoption, as the most direct road to their own object.

The zeal for attempts to amend, prior to the establishment of the Constitution, must abate in every man who is ready to accede to the truth of the following observations of a writer equally solid and ingenious: "To balance a large state or society (says he), whether monarchical or republican, on general laws, is a work of so great difficulty, that no human genius, however comprehensive, is able, by the mere dint of reason and reflection, to effect it. The judgments of many must unite in the work; experience must guide their labor; time must bring it to perfection, and the feeling of inconveniences must correct the mistakes which they *inevitably* fall into in their first trials and experiments."[8] These judicious reflections contain a lesson of moderation to all the sincere lovers of the Union, and ought to put them upon their guard against hazarding anarchy, civil war, a perpetual alienation of the states from each other, and perhaps the military despotism of a victorious demagogue, in the pursuit of what they are not likely to obtain, but from time and experience. It may be in me a defect of political fortitude, but I acknowledge that I cannot entertain an equal tranquility with those who affect to treat the dangers of a longer continuance in our present situation as imaginary. A nation, without a national government, is, in my view, an awful spectacle. The establishment of a Constitution, in time of profound peace, by the voluntary consent of a whole people, is a prodigy, to the completion of which I look forward with trembling anxiety. I can reconcile it to no rules of prudence to

---

[8] David Hume's *Essays,* Vol. I, page 128: "The Rise of Arts and Sciences." — *PUBLIUS.*

ON "ALTERING OUR FEDERAL GOVERNMENT": SPEECH BY PATRICK HENRY OF VIRGINIA

("My political curiosity, exclusive of my anxious solicitude for the public welfare, leads me to ask, Who authorized them to speak the language of 'We, the people,' instead of 'We, the states'?")

VIRGINIA RATIFYING CONVENTION
JUNE 4, 1788

Patrick Henry (1736–1799), a Revolutionary War hero and former governor of Virginia, was opposed to a centralized government from the start. He was the most eloquent of any of the speakers pro or con in Virginia, and overcoming his persuasiveness with voters took a concerted effort by Madison and others. On June 26, Virginia became the tenth state to ratify the Constitution, 88–79.

Mr. Chairman, the public mind, as well as my own, is extremely uneasy at the proposed change of government. Give me leave to form one of the number of those who wish to be thoroughly acquainted with the reasons of this perilous and uneasy situation, and why we are brought hither to decide on this great national question. I consider myself as the servant of the people of this commonwealth, as a sentinel over their rights, liberty, and happiness. I represent their feelings when I say that they are exceedingly uneasy at being brought from that state of full security, which they enjoyed, to the present delusive appearance of things. A year ago, the minds of our citizens were at perfect repose. Before the meeting of the late Federal Convention at Philadelphia, a general peace and a universal tranquility prevailed in this country; but, since that period, they are exceedingly uneasy and disquieted. When I wished for an appointment to this Convention, my mind was extremely agitated for the situation of public affairs. I conceived the republic to be in extreme danger. If our situation be thus uneasy, whence has arisen this fearful jeopardy? It arises from this fatal system;

139

it arises from a proposal to change our government—a proposal that goes to the utter annihilation of the most solemn engagements of the states—a proposal of establishing nine states into a confederacy, to the eventual exclusion of four states. It goes to the annihilation of those solemn treaties we have formed with foreign nations.

The present circumstances of France—the good offices rendered us by that kingdom—require our most faithful and most punctual adherence to our treaty with her. We are in alliance with the Spaniards, the Dutch, the Prussians; those treaties bound us as thirteen states confederated together. Yet here is a proposal to sever that confederacy. Is it possible that we shall abandon all our treaties and national engagements? And for what? I expected to hear the reasons for an event so unexpected to my mind and many others. Was our civil polity, or public justice, endangered or sapped? Was the real existence of the country threatened, or was this preceded by a mournful progression of events? This proposal of altering our federal government is of a most alarming nature! Make the best of this new government—say it is composed by anything but inspiration—you ought to be extremely cautious, watchful, jealous of your liberty; for, instead of securing your rights, you may lose them forever. If a wrong step be now made, the republic may be lost forever. If this new government will not come up to the expectation of the people, and they shall be disappointed, their liberty will be lost, and tyranny must and will arise. I repeat it again, and I beg gentlemen to consider, that a wrong step, made now, will plunge us into misery, and our republic will be lost.

It will be necessary for this Convention to have a faithful historical detail of the facts that preceded the session of the Federal Convention, and the reasons that actuated its members in proposing an entire alteration of government, and to demonstrate the dangers that awaited us. If they were of such awful magnitude as to warrant a proposal so extremely perilous as this, I must assert, that this Convention has an absolute right to a thorough discovery of every circumstance relative to this great event. And here I would make this inquiry of those worthy characters who composed a part of the late Federal Convention. I am sure they were fully impressed with the necessity of forming a great consolidated government, instead of a confederation. That this is a consolidated government is demonstrably clear; and the danger of such a government is, to my mind, very striking.

I have the highest veneration for those gentlemen; but, sir, give me leave to demand, What right had they to say, "We, the people"? My political curiosity, exclusive of my anxious solicitude for the public welfare, leads me to ask, Who authorized them to speak the language of "We, the people," instead of "We, the states"? States are the characteristics and the soul of a confederation. If the states be not the agents of this compact, it must be one great, consolidated, national government, of the people of all the states. I have the highest respect for those gentlemen who formed the Convention, and, were some of them not here, I would express some testimonial of esteem for them. America had, on a former occasion, put the utmost confidence in them—a confidence which was well placed; and I am sure, sir, I would give up any thing to them; I would cheerfully confide in them as my representatives. But, sir, on this great occasion, I would demand the cause of their conduct. Even from that illustrious man who saved us by his valor [*George Washington*], I would have a reason for his conduct: that liberty which he has given us by his valor, tells me to ask this reason; and sure I am, were he here, he would give us that reason. But there are other gentlemen here, who can give us this information.

The people gave them no power to use their name. That they exceeded their power is perfectly clear. It is not mere curiosity that actuates me: I wish to hear the real, actual, existing danger, which should lead us to take those steps, so dangerous in my conception. Disorders have arisen in other parts of America; but here, sir, no dangers, no insurrection or tumult have happened; everything has been calm and tranquil. But, notwithstanding this, we are wandering on the great ocean of human affairs. I see no landmark to guide us. We are running we know not whither. Difference of opinion has gone to a degree of inflammatory resentment in different parts of the country, which has been occasioned by this perilous innovation. The Federal Convention ought to have amended the old system; for this purpose they were solely delegated; the object of their mission extended to no other consideration. You must, therefore, forgive the solicitation of one unworthy member to know what danger could have arisen under the present Confederation, and what are the causes of this proposal to change our government.

DEBATE ON THE ABSENCE OF A BILL OF RIGHTS: JAMES MADISON AND PATRICK HENRY

("... I would declare it infinitely more safe, in its present form, than it would be after introducing into it that long train of alterations which they call amendments")

VIRGINIA RATIFYING CONVENTION
JUNE 24, 1788

With ratification close to assured, James Madison was able to calmly and clearly continue his advocacy for the Constitution in spite of Patrick Henry's angry denunciations.

MR. MADISON. Mr. Chairman, nothing has excited more admiration in the world than the manner in which free governments have been established in America; for it was the first instance, from the creation of the world to the American revolution, that free inhabitants have been seen deliberating on a form of government, and selecting such of their citizens as possessed their confidence, to determine upon and give effect to it. But why has this excited so much wonder and applause? Because it is of so much magnitude, and because it is liable to be frustrated by so many accidents. If it has excited so much wonder that the United States have, in the middle of war and confusion, formed free systems of government, how much more astonishment and admiration will be excited, should they be able peaceably, freely, and satisfactorily, to establish one general government, when there is such a diversity of opinions and interests—when not cemented or stimulated by any common danger! How vast must be the difficulty of concentrating, in one government, the interests, and conciliating the opinions, of so many different, heterogeneous bodies!

How have the confederacies of ancient and modern times been formed? As far as ancient history describes the former to us, they were brought about by the wisdom of some eminent sage. How was the imperfect union of the Swiss cantons formed? By danger. How was the confederacy of the United Netherlands formed? By the same. They are surrounded by dangers. By these, and one influential character, they were stimulated to unite. How was the Germanic system formed? By danger, in some degree, but principally by the overruling influence of individuals.

When we consider this government, we ought to make great allowances. We must calculate the impossibility that every state should be gratified in its wishes, and much less that every individual should receive this gratification. It has never been denied, by the friends of the paper on the table, that it has defects; but they do not think that it contains any real danger. They conceive that they will, in all probability, be removed, when experience will show it to be necessary. I beg that gentlemen, in deliberating on this subject, would consider the alternative. Either nine states shall have ratified it, or they will not. If nine states will adopt it, can it be reasonably presumed, or required, that nine states, having freely and fully considered the subject, and come to an affirmative decision, will, upon the demand of a single state, agree that they acted wrong, and could not see its defects — tread back the steps which they have taken, and come forward, and reduce it to uncertainty whether a general system shall be adopted or not? Virginia has always heretofore spoken the language of respect to the other states, and she has always been attended to. Will it be that language to call on a great majority of the states to acknowledge that they have done wrong? Is it the language of confidence to say that we do not believe that amendments for the preservation of the common liberty, and general interests, of the states, will be consented to by them? This is the language neither of confidence nor respect. Virginia, when she speaks respectfully, will be as much attended to as she has hitherto been when speaking this language

It is a most awful thing that depends on our decision — no less than whether the thirteen states shall unite freely, peaceably, and unanimously, for security of their common happiness and liberty, or whether every thing is to be put in confusion and disorder. Are we to embark in this dangerous enterprise, uniting various opinions to contrary interests, with the vain hope of coming to an amicable concurrence?

It is worthy of our consideration that those who prepared the paper on the table found difficulties not to be described in its formation: mutual deference and concession were absolutely necessary. Had they been inflexibly tenacious of their individual opinions, they would never have concurred. Under what circumstances was it formed?

When no party was formed, or particular proposition made, and men's minds were calm and dispassionate. Yet, under these circumstances, it was difficult, extremely difficult, to agree to any general system.

Suppose eight states only should ratify, and Virginia should propose certain alterations, as the previous condition of her accession. If they should be disposed to accede to her proposition, which is the most favorable conclusion, the difficulty attending it will be immense. Every state which has decided it, must take up the subject again. They must not only have the mortification of acknowledging that they had done wrong, but the difficulty of having a reconsideration of it among the people, and appointing new conventions to deliberate upon it. They must attend to *all* the amendments, which may be dictated by as great a diversity of political opinions as there are local attachments. When brought together in one assembly, they must go through, and accede to, every one of the amendments. The gentlemen who, within this house, have thought proper to propose previous amendments, have brought no less than forty amendments, a bill of rights which contains twenty amendments, and twenty other alterations, some of which are improper and inadmissible. Will not every state think herself equally entitled to propose as many amendments? And suppose them to be contradictory! I leave it to this Convention whether it be probable that they can agree, or agree to any thing but the plan on the table; or whether greater difficulties will not be encountered than were experienced in the progress of the formation of the Constitution.

I have said that there was a great contrariety of opinions among the gentlemen in the opposition. It has been heard in every stage of their opposition. I can see, from their amendments, that very great sacrifices have been made by some of them. Some gentlemen think that it contains too much state influence; others, that it is a complete consolidation; and a variety of other things. Some of them think that the equality in the Senate is not a defect; others, that it is the bane of all good government. I might, if there were time, show a variety of other cases where their opinions are contradictory. If there be this contrariety of opinions in this house, what contrariety may not be expected, when we take into view thirteen conventions equally or more numerous! Besides, it is notorious, from the debates which have been published, that there is no sort of uniformity in the grounds of the opposition.

The state of New York has been adduced. Many in that state are opposed to it from local views. The two who opposed it in the general Convention from that state are in the state Convention. Every step of this system was opposed by those two gentlemen. They were unwilling to part with the old Confederation. Can it be presumed, then, sir, that gentlemen in this state, who admit the necessity of changing, should ever be able to unite in sentiments with those who are totally averse to any change?

I have revolved this question in my mind with as much serious attention, and called to my aid as much information, as I could, yet I can see no reason for the apprehensions of gentlemen; but I think that the most happy effects for this country would result from adoption, and if Virginia will agree to ratify this system, I shall look upon it as one of the most fortunate events that ever happened for human nature. I cannot, therefore, without the most excruciating apprehensions, see a possibility of losing its blessings. It gives me infinite pain to reflect that all the earnest endeavors of the warmest friends of their country to introduce a system promotive of our happiness, may be blasted by a rejection, for which I think, with my honorable friend, that previous amendments are but another name. The gentlemen in opposition seem to insist on those amendments, as if they were all necessary for the liberty and happiness of the people. Were I to hazard an opinion on the subject, I would declare it infinitely more safe, in its present form, than it would be after introducing into it that long train of alterations which they call amendments.

With respect to the proposition of the honorable gentleman to my left *(Mr. Wythe)*, gentlemen apprehend that, by enumerating three rights, it implied there were no more. The observations made by a gentleman lately up, on that subject, correspond precisely with my opinion. That resolution declares that the powers granted by the proposed Constitution are the gift of the people, and may be resumed by them when perverted to their oppression, and every power not granted thereby remains with the people, and at their will. It adds, likewise, that no right, of any denomination, can be cancelled, abridged, restrained, or modified, by the general government, or any of its officers, except in those instances in which power is given by the Constitution for these purposes. There cannot be a more positive and unequivocal declaration of the principle of the adoption — that every thing not granted is reserved. This is obviously and self-evidently the case, without the declaration. Can the general government exercise any power not delegated? If an enumeration be made of our rights, will it not be implied that every thing omitted is given to the general government? Has not the honorable gentleman himself admitted that an imperfect enumeration is dangerous? Does the Constitution say that they shall not alter the law of descents, or do those things which would subvert the whole system of the state laws? If it did, what was not excepted would be granted. Does it follow, from the omission of such restrictions, that they can exercise powers not delegated? The reverse of the proposition holds. The delegation alone warrants the exercise of any power.

With respect to *the amendments* proposed by the honorable gentleman, it ought to be considered how far they are good. As far as they are palpably and insuperably objectionable, they ought to be opposed. One amendment he proposes is, that any army which shall be necessary shall be raised by the consent of two thirds of the states. I most devoutly wish that there may never be an occasion for having a single regiment. There can be no harm in declaring that standing armies, in time of peace, are dangerous to liberty, and ought to be avoided, as far as it may be consistent with the protection of the community. But when we come to say that the national security shall depend, not on a majority of the people of America, but that it may be frustrated by less than one third of the people of America, I ask if this be a safe or proper mode. What parts of the United States are most likely to stand in need of this protection? The weak parts, which are the Southern states. Will it be safe to leave the United States at the mercy of one third of the states—a number which may comprise a very small proportion of the American people? They may all be in that part of America which is least exposed to danger. As far as a remote situation from danger would render exertions for public defence less active, so far the Southern states would be endangered.

The regulation of *commerce,* he further proposed, should depend on two thirds of both houses. I wish I could recollect the history of this matter; but I cannot call it to mind with sufficient exactness. But I well recollect the reasoning of some gentlemen on that subject. It was said, and I believe with truth, that every part of America does not stand in equal need of security. It was observed that the Northern states were most competent to their own safety. Was it reasonable, asked they, that they should bind themselves to the defense of the Southern states, and still be left at the mercy of the minority for commercial advantages? Should it be in the power of the minority to deprive them of this and other advantages, when they were bound to defend the whole Union, it might be a disadvantage for them to confederate.

These were his arguments. This policy of guarding against political inconveniences, by enabling a small part of the community to oppose the government, and subjecting the majority to a small minority, is fallacious. In some cases it may be good; in others it may be fatal. In all cases, it puts it in the power of the minority to decide a question which concerns the majority.

I was struck with surprise when I heard him express himself alarmed with respect to the emancipation of slaves. Let me ask, if they should even attempt it, if it will not be a usurpation of power. There is no power to warrant it, in that paper. If there be, I know it not. But why should it be done? Says the honorable gentleman, for the general welfare: it will infuse strength into our system. Can any member of this committee suppose that it will increase our strength? Can any one believe that the American councils will come into a measure which will strip them of their property, and discourage and alienate the affections of five thirteenths of the Union? Why was nothing of this sort aimed at before? I believe such an idea never entered into any American breast, nor do I believe it ever will enter into the heads of those gentlemen who substitute unsupported suspicions for reasons.

I am persuaded that the gentlemen who contend for previous amendments are not aware of the dangers which must result. Virginia, after having made opposition, will be obliged to recede from it. Might not the nine states say, with a great deal of propriety, "It is not proper, decent, or right, in you, to demand that we should reverse what we have done. Do as we have done; place confidence in us, as we have done in one another; and then we shall freely, fairly, and dispassionately consider and investigate your propositions, and endeavor to gratify your wishes. But if you do not do this, it is more reasonable that you should yield to us than we to you. You cannot exist without us; you must be a member of the Union."

The case of Maryland, instanced by the gentleman, does not hold. She would not agree to confederate, because the other states would not assent to her claims of the western lands. Was she gratified? No; she put herself like the rest. Nor has she since been gratified. The lands are in the common stock of the Union.

As far as his amendments are not objectionable, or unsafe, so far they may be subsequently recommended—not because they are necessary, but because they can produce no possible danger, and may gratify some gentlemen's wishes. But I never can consent to his previous amendments, because they are pregnant with dreadful dangers.

MR. HENRY. Mr. Chairman, the honorable gentleman who was up some time ago exhorts us not to fall into a repetition of the defects of the Confederation. He said we ought not to declare that each state retains every power jurisdiction, and right, which is not expressly delegated, because experience has proved the insertion of such a restriction to be destructive, and mentioned an instance to prove it. That case, Mr. Chairman, appears to me to militate against himself. Passports would not be given by Congress—and why? Because there was a clause in the Confederation which denied them implied powers. And says he, Shall we repeat the error? He asked me where was the power of emancipating slaves. I say it will be implied, unless implication be prohibited. He admits that the power of granting passports will be in the new Congress without the insertion of this restriction; yet he can show me nothing like such a power granted in that Constitution. Notwithstanding he admits their right to this power by implication, he says that I am unfair and uncandid in my deduction that they can emancipate our slaves, though the word *emancipation* is not mentioned in it. They can exercise power by implication in one instance, as well as in another. Thus, by the gentleman's own argument, they can exercise the power, though it be not delegated.

We were then told that the power of treaties and commerce was the *sine qua non* of the Union; that the little states would not confederate otherwise. There is a thing not present to human view. We have seen great concessions from the large states to the little states. But little concessions from the little states to the great states will be refused. He concedes that great concessions were made in the great Convention. Now, when we speak of rights, and not of emoluments, these little states would not have been affected. What boon did we ask? We demanded only rights which ought to be unalienable and sacred. We have nothing local to ask. We ask rights which concern the general happiness. Must not justice bring them into the concession of these? The honorable gentleman was pleased to say that the new government, in this policy, will be equal to what the present is. If so, that amendment will not injure that part.

He then mentioned the danger that would arise from foreign gold. We may be bribed by foreign powers if we ask for amendments, to secure our own happiness. Are we to be bribed to forget our own interests? I will ask, if foreign gold be likely to operate, where will it be? In the seat of government, or in those little channels in which the state authority will flow? It will be at the fountain of power, where bribery will not be detected. He speaks of war and bloodshed. Whence do this war and bloodshed come? I fear it, but not from the source he speaks of. I fear it, sir, from the operation and friends of the federal government. He speaks with contempt of this amendment. But whoever will advert to the use made repeatedly, in England, of the prerogative of the king, and the frequent attacks on the privileges of the people, notwithstanding many legislative acts to secure them, will see the necessity of excluding implications. Nations who have trusted to logical deduction have lost their liberty.

The honorable gentleman last up agrees that there are defects, and by and by, he says there is no defect. Does not this amount to a declaration that subsequent amendments are not necessary? His arguments, great as the gentleman's abilities are, tend to prove that amendments cannot be obtained after adoption. Speaking of forty amendments, he calculated that it was something like impracticability to obtain them. I appeal, therefore, to the candor of the honorable gentleman, and this committee, whether amendments be not absolutely unattainable, if we adopt; for he has told us that, if the other states will do like this, they cannot be previously obtained. Will the gentleman bring this home to himself? This is a piece of information which I expected. The worthy member who proposed to ratify has also proposed that what amendments may be deemed necessary should be recommended to Congress, and that a committee should be appointed to consider what amendments were necessary. But what does it all come to at last? That it is a vain project, and that it is indecent and improper. I will not argue unfairly, but I will ask him if amendments are not unattainable. Will gentlemen, then, lay their hands on their hearts, and say that they can adopt it in this shape? When we demand this security of our privileges, the language of Virginia is not that of respect! Give me leave to deny. She only asks amendments previous to her adoption of the Constitution.

Was the honorable gentleman accurate, when he said that they could exist better without us than we could without them? I will make no comparison. But I will say that the states which have adopted will not make a respectable appearance without us. Would he advise them to refuse us admission when we profess ourselves friends to the Union, and only solicit them to secure our rights? We do not reject a connection with them. We only declare that we will adopt it, if they will but consent to the security of rights essential to the general happiness.

He told you to confine yourselves to amendments which were indisputably true, as applying to several parts of the system proposed. Did you hear any thing like the admission of the want of such amendments from any one else? I will not insist on any that does not stand on the broad basis of human rights. He says there are forty. I say there is but one half the number, for the bill of rights is but one amendment.

He tells you of the important blessings which he imagines will result to us and mankind in general from the adoption of this system. I see the awful immensity of the dangers with which it is pregnant. I see it. I feel it. I see beings of a higher order anxious concerning our decision. When I see beyond the horizon that bounds human eyes, and look at the final consummation of all human things, and see those intelligent beings which inhabit the ethereal mansions reviewing the political decisions and revolutions which, in the progress of time, will happen in America, and the consequent happiness or misery of mankind, I am led to believe that much of the account, on one side or the other, will depend on what we now decide. Our own happiness alone is not affected by the event. All nations are interested in the determination. We have it in our power to secure the happiness of one half of the human race. Its adoption may involve the misery of the other hemisphere.

(Here a violent storm arose, which put the house in such disorder, that MR. HENRY *was obliged to conclude.)*

MR. NICHOLAS proposed that the question should be put at nine o'clock next day.

He was opposed by MR. CLAY.

MR. RONALD also opposed the motion, and wished amendments to he prepared by a committee, before the question should be put.

MR. NICHOLAS contended that the language of the proposed ratification would secure every thing which gentlemen desired, as it declared that all powers vested in the Constitution were derived from the people, and might be resumed by them whensoever they should be perverted to their injury and oppression; and that every power not granted thereby remained at their will. No danger whatever could arise; for, says he, these expressions will become a part of the contract. The Constitution cannot be binding on Virginia, but with these conditions. If thirteen individuals are about to make a contract, and one agrees to it, but at the same time declares that he understands its meaning, signification, and intent, to be (what the words of the contract plainly and obviously denote), that it is not to be construed so as to impose any supplementary condition upon him, and that he is to be exonerated from it whensoever any such imposition shall be attempted,—I ask whether, in this case, these conditions, on which he has assented to it, would not be binding on the other twelve. In like manner these conditions will be binding on Congress. They can exercise no power that is not expressly granted them.

MR. RONALD. Mr. Chairman, I came hither with a determination to give my vote so as to secure the liberty and privileges of my constituents. I thought that a great majority argued that amendments were necessary. Such is my opinion; but whether they ought to be previous or subsequent to our adoption, I leave to the wisdom of this committee to determine. I feel an earnest desire to know what amendments shall be proposed, before the question be put. One honorable gentleman has proposed several amendments. They are objected to by other gentlemen. I do not declare myself for or against those amendments; but unless I see such amendments, one way or the other, introduced, as will secure the happiness of the people, and prevent their privileges from being endangered, I must, though much against my inclination, vote against this Constitution.

MR. MADISON conceived that what defects might be in the Constitution might be removed by the amendatory mode in itself. As to a solemn declaration of our essential rights, he thought it unnecessary and dangerous—unnecessary, because it was evident that the general government had no power but what was given it, and that the delegation alone warranted the exercise of power; dangerous, because an enumeration which is not complete is not safe. Such an enumeration could not be made, within any compass of time, as would be equal to a general negation, such as his honorable friend *(Mr. Wythe)* had proposed. He declared that such amendments as seemed, in his judgment, to be without danger, he would readily admit, and that he would be the last to oppose any such amendment as would give satisfaction to any gentleman, unless it were dangerous.

THE BILL OF RIGHTS

DECEMBER 15, 1791

> *What was and continues to be known as the "Bill of Rights" are the first ten amendments to the Constitution. The pervasive call for their inclusion during the state conventions on the Constitution's ratification made these amendments an essential supplement to that document.*

Preamble

Congress of the United States begun and held at the City of New-York, on Wednesday the fourth of March, one thousand seven hundred and eighty nine.

The Conventions of a number of the States, having at the time of their adopting the Constitution, expressed a desire, in order to prevent misconstruction or abuse of its powers, that further declaratory and restrictive clauses should be added: And as extending the ground of public confidence in the Government, will best ensure the beneficent ends of its institution.

Resolved by the Senate and House of Representatives of the United States of America, in Congress assembled, two thirds of both Houses concurring, that the following Articles be proposed to the Legislatures of the several States, as amendments to the Constitution of the United States, all, or any of which Articles, when ratified by three fourths of the said Legislatures, to be valid to all intents and purposes, as part of the said Constitution; viz.

ARTICLES in addition to, and Amendment of the Constitution of the United States of America, proposed by Congress, and ratified by the Legislatures of the several States, pursuant to the fifth Article of the original Constitution.

Amendment I

Congress shall make no law respecting an establishment of religion, or prohibiting the free exercise thereof; or abridging the freedom of speech, or of the press; or the right of the people peaceably to assemble, and to petition the Government for a redress of grievances.

Amendment II

A well regulated Militia, being necessary to the security of a free State, the right of the people to keep and bear Arms, shall not be infringed.

Amendment III

No Soldier shall, in time of peace be quartered in any house, without the consent of the Owner, nor in time of war, but in a manner to be prescribed by law.

Amendment IV

The right of the people to be secure in their persons, houses, papers, and effects, against unreasonable searches and seizures, shall not be violated, and no Warrants shall issue, but upon probable cause, supported by Oath or affirmation, and particularly describing the place to be searched, and the persons or things to be seized.

Amendment V

No person shall be held to answer for a capital, or otherwise infamous crime, unless on a presentment or indictment of a Grand Jury, except in cases arising in the land or naval forces, or in the Militia, when in actual service in time of War or public danger; nor shall any person be subject for the same offence to be twice put in jeopardy of life or limb; nor shall be compelled in any criminal case to be a witness against himself, nor be deprived of life, liberty, or property, without due process of law; nor shall private property be taken for public use, without just compensation.

Amendment VI

In all criminal prosecutions, the accused shall enjoy the right to a speedy and public trial, by an impartial jury of the State and district wherein the crime shall have been committed, which district shall have been previously ascertained by law, and to be informed of the nature and cause of the accusation; to be confronted with the witnesses against him; to have compulsory process for obtaining witnesses in his favor, and to have the Assistance of Counsel for his defence.

Amendment VII

In Suits at common law, where the value in controversy shall exceed twenty dollars, the right of trial by jury shall be preserved, and no fact tried by a jury, shall be otherwise re-examined in any Court of the United States, than according to the rules of the common law.

Amendment VIII

Excessive bail shall not be required, nor excessive fines imposed, nor cruel and unusual punishments inflicted.

Amendment IX

The enumeration in the Constitution, of certain rights, shall not be construed to deny or disparage others retained by the people.

Amendment X

The powers not delegated to the United States by the Constitution, nor prohibited by it to the States, are reserved to the States respectively, or to the people.